P9-CPX-830

The Church of the New Testament

...BY...

C. J. SHARP

Bro Bob Graham

The Standard Press

THE STANDARD PUBLISHING COMPANY

CINCINNATI, OHIO, U.S.A.

The quotations that are used in this book from the American Standard Edition of the Revised Bible, copyright, 1929, by International Council of Religious Education, are used by permission.

Printed in U. S. A.

Foreword

This volume is planned and intended to be a frank presentation of the church as it is definitely pictured in the New Testament. The plan of the book is that all important phases and features of the church be logically grouped under the twenty chapter heads, and that each of the phases be presented by means of a generous use of the Scriptures.

The author has labored to present the whole matter briefly, yet clearly. Much more could easily be added to each and every chapter and to every paragraph, but that would immediately defeat the purposes of brevity, simplicity and economy. We hope, however, that enough has been given to make each subject treated not only plain, but conclusive.

The book is intended as a study book for workers, a handbook for ministers and a book of vital information for all Christians for study purposes. It is not intended as a controversial treatise on controverted subjects, though many of the subjects treated have been the source of much controversy. We have made little or no attempt, except in one or two cases, even to call attention to later departures from the New Testament pattern. Where we have so referred, it is done merely for illustration that the New Testament plan may stand out by contrast. We believe that the New Testament plainly presents the pattern of the church. Our effort is, therefore, to set forth the plan as given by the Spirit of God and leave the divine Word to accomplish that whereto God has sent it. —THE AUTHOR.

Contents

6 *Contents*

Chapter I

What Is Meant by the Church of the New Testament?

I. THE CHURCH OF WHICH CHRIST SPOKE

(Read Matt. 16 : 15-20.)

This course is to be a study of the church of the New Testament. It is well in the very beginning to make clear what we mean by the term. We mean that church of which Christ spoke when He said, "On this rock will I build my church." There are apparently so many churches and kinds of churches today that confusion in the minds of people is bound to obtain. We can disregard and dismiss this confusion, however, if we can positively find, identify and understand the church which Christ, the one and only Saviour, said He would build.

1. Inspired References to the Church.—Paul and other New Testament writers refer many times, indeed, to "the church," "the churches of Christ," "the church of the living God," etc. These inspired men learned from Jesus Himself.

2. Jesus Pictures the Church Under the Title of "The Kingdom."—In addition, Jesus referred to the church over one hundred times under the title of "the kingdom." * Under this title He gave a quite complete picture of "the kingdom" as to its nature, its work, its purpose, its extent and its peculiarities. It is, therefore, of this church of Christ (Christ's

---

* NOTE—The terms "kingdom" and "kingdom of heaven" are synonymous, but are used in the New Testament in two senses—the kingdom on earth (the church) and the eternal kingdom (in heaven).

church as described in the New Testament) that we treat and refer to as "the church of the New Testament."

II. THE CHURCH OF WHICH CHRIST IS THE SOLE HEAD

It must be borne in mind that this New Testament church is one of which Christ is to be the sole and only Head on earth as well as in heaven. This is made abundantly plain by many Scriptures:

And hath put all things under his feet, and gave him to be the head over all things to the church, which is his body, the fulness of him that filleth all in all.—Eph. 1: 22, 23.

For the husband is the head of the wife, even as Christ is the head of the church: and he is the saviour of the body.—Eph. 5: 23.

But speaking the truth in love, may grow up into him in all things, which is the head, even Christ.—Eph. 4: 15.

And he is the head of the body, the church: who is the beginning, the first-born from the dead; that in all things he might have the pre-eminence. Who now rejoice in my sufferings for you, and fill up that which is behind of the afflictions of Christ in my flesh for his body's sake, which is the church.—Col. 1: 18, 24.

See also John 3: 31-36.

From the above Scriptures and others that could be cited, it becomes plain that the New Testament church has but *one* head and that head is Christ. There is no provision left for an earthly head or heads.

III. THE CHURCH OF WHICH CHRIST IS THE CHIEF CORNERSTONE

The chief Cornerstone of the New Testament church is Christ, not some one passage of Scripture, not some one dogma or theology or creed. Again the Scriptures make the matter plain.

Unto you therefore which believe he is precious: but unto them which be disobedient, the stone which the builders disallowed, the same is made the head of the corner.—1 Pet. 2: 7.

See also Acts 4: 11.

And are built upon the foundation of the apostles and prophets, Jesus Christ himself being the chief corner stone.—Eph. 2: 20.

For other foundation can no man lay than that is laid, which is Jesus Christ.—1 Cor. 3: 11.

These and other Scriptures make plain that Christ, the Son of the living God, is the Foundation of the church, as well as the chief Cornerstone. When He said, "On this *rock* will I build my church," He referred to the great foundational truth which Peter had just uttered, "Thou art the Christ, the Son of the living God." The Holy Spirit, who gave us the New Testament, left no excuse for following men to the point of dividing the church. Luther, Calvin, Wesley, Rogers, Campbell and such were but men. No one of them was or could be the Saviour. Paul disparages the following of Paul or Apollos or Peter to the dividing of the church (1 Cor. 1: 11-13).

IV. THE CHURCH WHICH IS TO BE THE BRIDE OF CHRIST
(John 3: 28-31; Rev. 22: 17.)

The New Testament church is likened to a bride. Christ is the Bridegroom. Two things are thus established. First, the church should stand for things that are pure, good and holy at all times and in all places. It is not an institution of rituals through which open and continued sin may be wiped out by ritualistic observances. The church of Christ ever opposes sin rather than to condone and profit therefrom. Second, the bride should wear the Bridegroom's name. The bride to which John alludes in the reference above is the church.

V. THE CHURCH WHICH IS THE BODY OF CHRIST

As Christ is the Head, the church is the body, Christ's body. The members of the church are each members of the body.

And he is the head of the body, the church.—Col. 1: 18.

For no man ever yet hated his own flesh; but nourisheth and cherisheth it, even as the Lord the church: for we are members of his body, of his flesh, and of his bones.—Eph. 5: 29, 30.

And he gave some, apostles; and some, prophets; and some, evangelists; and some, pastors and teachers; for the perfecting of the saints, for the work of the ministry, for the edifying of the body of Christ.—Eph. 4: 11, 12.

Men have too often assumed that the church belongs to ecclesiastical leaders and church potentates. Shall men not answer to God if they allow personal ambition and party prejudice to lead to the dividing and rending of the body of Christ? It is and should be *one* body just as there is and should be *one* head.

VI. The Church of Which Christ Is the Sole Owner.

The most important point of this chapter is that *the church is Christ's*. He owns it. It belongs to Him and to Him alone. He bought it with His blood. He is the Head, the Founder, the Designer, the *Owner*.

If the church were ours, we could do what we might wish with it. We could change its name to suit our fancy, or change its ordinances to suit our convenience. But since it is Christ's and inasmuch as He never commissioned any man or group of men, since the days of the apostles, to add to or take from the plans and specifications laid down in the New Testament, we can learn of His church only from the New Testament. The Holy Spirit gave us the New Testament through divinely inspired men. We must keep in mind that Christ sent the Holy Spirit.

Take heed therefore unto yourselves, and to all the flock, over the which the Holy Ghost hath made you overseers, to feed the church of God, which he hath purchased with his own blood.—Acts 20: 28.

Read again Matt. 16: 18.

VII. Summary.

To summarize all that has been said in this chapter, let us have clearly in mind that the New Testament church is a *divine institution.* It is the one and only divine institution. The church of the New Testament is:

1. Divine in its *origin*.
2. Divine in its *ownership*.
3. Divine in its *purpose*.
4. Divine in its *plan*.
5. Divine in its *name*.
6. Divine in its *guidance*.

These truths are basic and fundamental and are ever to be kept in mind as we proceed to a study of the New Testament church.

QUESTIONS

1. Of what church did Christ speak when He designated the foundation on which He would build it?

2. How does the multiplicity of churches today tend to confuse the unsaved?

3. In what two senses is the term "kingdom" or "kingdom of heaven" used in the New Testament? Which of these is synonymous with the church?

4. Who is the one and only Head of the New Testament church?

5. Quote or summarize some Scriptures showing that Christ is the one Head of the church.

6. What do we learn about the church from the Scriptural figures of speech, "chief corner stone" and "foundation"?

7. What two things may we learn about the church from the figure, "the bride of Christ"?

8. Does the New Testament picture many bodies of Christ or *one* body and *one* Head?

9. Who are the members of the body?

Answer. All individual Christians constitute the members of His body.

10. Who owns the church?

11. Since Christ established the church and owns it wholly, who may change it?

12. Name six respects in which the church is a divine institution.

13. Have any human beings the right to change things divinely established?

Chapter II

Preparation for the Founding of the Church

I. PREPARATIONS IN FORMER DISPENSATIONS

It should be kept in mind that the "church of Christ," the "New Testament church" and the "kingdom of Christ" are used synonymously in many passages. Unquestionably, the following passage from the prophet Isaiah refers to the kingdom of Christ or the world-wide reign of Christ, the assembly of Christ, the church of Christ:

For unto us a child is born, unto us a son is given: and the government shall be upon his shoulder: and his name shall be called Wonderful, Counsellor, The mighty God, The everlasting Father, The Prince of Peace. Of the increase of his government and peace there shall be no end, upon the throne of David, and upon his kingdom, to order it, and to establish it with judgment and with justice from henceforth even for ever.—Isa. 9: 6, 7.

Again, the following Scripture from Daniel unquestionably refers to the world-wide spread of the kingdom of Christ, the church of Christ:

Thou sawest till that a stone was cut out without hands, which smote the image upon his feet that were of iron and clay, and brake them to pieces . . . and the stone that smote the image became a great mountain, and filled the whole earth.—Dan. 2: 34, 35.*

The Old Testament is packed with prophesyings, foreshadowings and preparations for the coming of the Christ and His kingdom. All the Old Testament history, including that in Genesis, is built around the history of one family and they the

---

* It is suggested that the entire second chapter of Daniel be read in this connection.

progenitors of Christ. Hundreds of prophecies might be cited. Isaiah is so filled with specific and minute prophecies about Christ that he has been called "the gospel prophet." All the foretellings about the coming King and coming kingdom look toward the Christ and His church.

II. FORESHADOWINGS IN THE OLD TESTAMENT

While the subject is too large to treat at length in a paragraph, yet we may call to mind that the very acts of worship of the Mosaic dispensation were largely types of the perfect order which was to come. For example, the lamb slain was a type of Christ, the Lamb of God. The high priest, mediator for man with God, was a type of "the great High Priest," Jesus the Lord, who was to come. The burning incense was typical of ever ascending Christian prayer. The laver and its washing was a type of the cleansing through the blood of Christ. We might go on to great length to show these Old Testament types of Christian procedures, but enough has been said to make plain that the church in all its phases and significance was foreshadowed, pictured and prophesied through the many centuries before the church existed as the body of Christ.

III. FOUNDATIONAL TEACHINGS IN THE NEW TESTAMENT

While the church was not established until Pentecost after the resurrection and ascension of Jesus; while the history of this first beginning of the church is recorded in Acts; while it is true that Jesus' life on earth and the events recorded in the Gospels took place in the Mosaic dispensation, yet it is true that the definite and final *preparation* for the founding of the church is recorded in the Gospels. It is here that the principles of the kingdom are laid down in Jesus' teaching. The proofs of His divine Sonship are given through His acts, teachings, death and resurrection. Those into whose hands He planned to entrust the actual founding of the church were chosen, trained and instructed. The Holy Spirit as a divine Guide was promised. The church could not be founded and based on Christ as the Son of the living God until the last, final and unanswerable proof of His divine Sonship had been given. The final proof was His resurrection.

Again, may we call to mind that Jesus' much teaching about the kingdom as recorded in the Gospels leaves no room for doubt as to its principles, purposes and general plan. All this was in preparation for the founding of His church. The many parables about the kingdom pictured the church in its every phase and significance. Read any of the parables which begin, "The kingdom of heaven is like unto," etc.

IV. Prophecies and Promises in the New Testament

Most of the New Testament promises and prophecies about the church are contained in the Gospels or in Revelation. Those in the Gospels almost entirely look toward things shortly to be done or fulfilled. Most of those in Revelation look toward the far future consummation of things pertaining to the church. All through the Gospels the church is discussed as something *to come,* something that was *near at hand.* After Pentecost the church is referred to by all New Testament writers as something then in existence. As examples of a few of the promises and prophecies, note the following:

And upon this rock I will build my church.—Matt. 16: 18.

But the Comforter, which is the Holy Ghost, whom the Father will send in my name, he shall teach you all things, and bring all things to your remembrance, whatsoever I have said unto you.—John 14: 26.

Howbeit when he, the Spirit of truth, is come, he will guide you into all truth.—John 16: 13.

But tarry ye in the city of Jerusalem, until ye be endued with power from on high.—Luke 24: 49.

I will give unto thee the keys of the kingdom of heaven: and whatsoever thou shalt bind on earth shall be bound in heaven.*—Matt. 16: 19.

---

* Spoken to Peter.

V. THE CHURCH AND THE KINGDOM

1. The Term "Kingdom" Frequently Used as a Synonym for "the Church."—In former paragraphs, attention has been called to the fact that in both Old and New Testaments the terms "kingdom" and "kingdom of God" are used to refer to or as synonymous with "the church" (Eph. 5 : 23) ; "church of God" (Acts 20 : 28) ; "the church of the. living God" (1 Tim. 3 : 15) ; "the body of Christ" (Col. 1 : 24) ; "the churches of Christ" (Rom. 16 : 16). In order to understand and appreciate the abundant teaching about the church in both Old and New Testaments, it is essential that this fact be kept in mind.

2. Attempts to Make a Distinction.—There are some who have attempted to draw a line of distinction between the two and to make of the "kingdom" something more extensive than and different from the church. To do so only confuses what are otherwise plain Scripture teachings. Jesus said to Peter : "On this rock will I build my *church* . . . and I will give unto thee the keys of the kingdom of heaven," etc. On Pentecost, Peter used these keys and what he unlocked and threw open was the church. Bear in mind that there is not a principle taught by Christ in regard to the kingdom which is not enjoined on Christians as members of Christ's church. The members of one are citizens of the other. Matthew refers to it as "the kingdom of heaven." Mark and Luke call it the "kingdom of God." Paul refers to it as "the church of God." (1 Cor. 15 : 9 ; Gal. 1 : 13 ; 1 Tim. 3 : 15.) But at Corinth, Paul was reasoning and persuading as to the things concerning "the kingdom of God" (Acts 19 : 8). At Rome he expounded and testified "the kingdom of God," persuading them concerning Jesus, both out of the law of Moses and out of the prophets, from morning to night. What was Paul doing but preaching and teaching to win people and make them Christians and members of the church? Evidently he used both of the terms for the same institution.

VI. Preparation of Leaders for the Founding of the Church

Little need be said on the subject of preparation of the leaders into whose hands the founding of the church was to be entrusted. Most of that has been anticipated in the foregoing paragraphs. Recall that out of the many who believed in Him and followed Him at one time or another He chose twelve whom He kept with Him for three years. These He taught, and before their eyes He performed all His wonderful works. These He made witnesses of His death and His resurrection. To them He sent the Holy Spirit to endue, inspire and guide them that they might with divine guidance do the task He entrusted to them. This was His last act in preparation for the founding of the New Testament church, His church, the church of Christ.

QUESTIONS

1. What can you say of preparation for the founding of the church of Christ as shown in the Old Testament?

2. Can you give some examples of prophecies that were made about this coming kingdom or church?

3. Why is Isaiah called "the gospel prophet"?

4. Name some of the features of Jewish worship which were types of Christ and Christian practice and worship.

5. When was the church started, and in what book of the New Testament is the record given?

6. What place do the records in the Gospels fill, looking toward the founding of the church?

7. Name some of the things recorded in the Gospels which were in direct preparation for the founding of the church.

8. What tense is used in the Gospels when referring to the founding of the church? Give examples.

9. Give some Scriptures showing "the church" and "the kingdom" to be the same.

10. In what ways did Jesus prepare His immediate followers for their task in founding the church?

11. What was His last preparatory act?

Chapter III

Necessary Preparation Before the Church Could Be Founded

I. OLD TESTAMENT PREPARATION FOR THE COMING OF CHRIST

1. Preparing a People.—From the very beginning the records of the Old Testament are the records of God's preparation of a people through whom the Redeemer and His gospel might be given to the world.

2. Proofs Through Which Jesus Might Be Recognized as the Son of God.—Literally hundreds of minute prophecies are scattered through the Old Testament, from Genesis to Malachi, which lay a perfect groundwork for the recognition of the Messiah when He should come. In fact, a quite complete biography of Jesus could be constructed from the prophecies of the Old Testament. These were written through a period of eleven hundred years, the last ones dating four hundred years before Christ's advent. When this groundwork had been completed Jesus came, fulfilling these prophecies and thus identifying Himself as the divine Son of God, sent from God, the promised Messiah.

II. JESUS' INCARNATION A NECESSARY PREPARATION

It is impossible for finite man to comprehend God. It is logical, therefore, to presume that we may never in this world fully understand all that is implied and comprehended in the incarnation. We can understand the Scriptural statement that God saw fit to come to earth in the form of His Son and clothed in the flesh of men to dwell among men, be "tempted in all things, like as we are tempted," suffer as we suffer and thus stoop to lift up fallen man.

III. That Jesus Should Live a Perfect Life

In deity there is room for no imperfection. The one thing on which all hinges is the answer to the question, Is this Jesus the Son of the living God? If so, the life He lived and the teaching He gave must be perfect, flawless, faultless. For thirty-three years He lived and walked among men, and lived a life and left teaching in which through twenty centuries not even His bitterest enemies have been able to establish one flaw. In this He is unique. There is none other. Christ's perfect life and teaching become two of the proofs of His deity.

IV. That Jesus Should Die

"Apart from shedding of blood there is no remission" (Heb. 9:22, A.R.V.). Again, only the wisdom of God can wholly comprehend why Jesus must die. Here, faith is required on our part. "The blood of Jesus Christ, his Son, cleanseth us from all sin" is a part of the mystery of which Paul speaks. If we believe the Bible to be the Word of God, however, we believe the fact stated, and to that extent we may understand why the Saviour must die and why that was a necessary preparation for the founding of the church.

V. That Jesus Should Come Forth Alive

1. Only by Entering the Grave Could Jesus Triumph Over It.—The church is built on Jesus as the Christ, the Son of God. He said, "On this rock will I build my church," i. e., on the truth that He was more than a perfect man, more than the wisest of teachers, that He was indeed God's own and only begotten Son. This was the final test. That test could be completed only by a demonstration of His complete power over death, yea over *His own death*. The resurrection constituted that final demonstration. Only by entering the gates of death could He come forth as victor over death.

2. What the Church Cost.—When we consider the church lightly we entirely overlook what it cost that the church of Christ might even be launched. When we look upon the church as merely one of the good world organizations, comparing it with other institutions of the world, we have wholly failed to understand that the church is the only *divine* institution.

3. The Church a Unique Institution.—The church is unique, it stands alone. It is the one and only institution of which God is the sponsor, Christ the head, and which has for its purpose salvation. Christ alone brings to mankind not only a code of ethics, not only forgiveness of sin, but eternal life. Said Jesus, "No man cometh unto the Father, but by me." There is no other way. This is what the church, His church, means. Before such a church could be founded it was necessary that Jesus should demonstrate not only His love, but His power to fulfill His promise of life everlasting in the face of universal death.

VI. Choosing and Training of the Apostles

Another preparation for the founding of the church by Jesus was the choosing of the men into whose hands He should commit the actual work of founding the church when He had completed all necessary preparations. These men, as we know, were the apostles, including Paul.

As incompletely as these men understood His mission and message, even to the very time of the resurrection, yet, in these years of sifting and teaching, He had prepared them as fit vessels into whom the Holy Spirit might be poured. One mission of the Holy Spirit was to call to their minds all He had taught them as well as to guide them into all truth.

VII. The Sending of the Holy Spirit

The final preparation for the founding of the church was the sending of the Holy Spirit to fill and guide these chosen men. Men, as such, however taught and however sincere, are yet fallible. To found the church of Christ and to give the gospel of Christ to the world called for divine guidance. This, Jesus promised and this He fulfilled.

If ye love me, keep my commandments. And I will pray the Father, and he shall give you another Comforter, that he may abide with you for ever; even the Spirit of truth; whom the world cannot receive, because it seeth him not, neither knoweth him: but ye know him; for he dwelleth with you, and shall be in you.—John 14: 15-17.

Nevertheless I tell you the truth; It is expedient for you that I go away: for if I go not away, the Comforter will not come unto you; but if I depart, I will send him unto you. . . . Howbeit when he, the Spirit of truth, is come, he will guide you into all truth: for he shall not speak of himself; but whatsoever he shall hear, that shall he speak: and he will shew you things to come.—John 16: 7-13.

Which things also we speak, not in the words which man's wisdom teacheth, but which the Holy Ghost teacheth; comparing spiritual things with spiritual.—1 Cor. 2: 13.

QUESTIONS

1. What definite preparations for the founding of the church are made in the Old Testament?

2. How do these Old Testament promises and prophecies help to identify the Christ?

3. In what way was the incarnation a preparation for the founding of the church?

4. Why was it necessary that Jesus should live a perfect life and leave perfect teaching on earth?

5. Why was Jesus' death a necessary essential to the founding of His church? Can we expect to understand all the reasons?

6. What relationship does the resurrection of Jesus have to the proofs of His deity?

7. How does the resurrection help to explain the necessity for His death?

8. How did Jesus prepare His apostles for their part in founding the church?

9. Why was it necessary that the Holy Spirit be sent to these chosen and taught men?

10. What was the Holy Spirit's mission?

Chapter IV

The Relation of the Gospels to the Church

I. Churches to Be Founded Through All Time

While it is true that the church was founded and launched before the Gospels were written, it is also true that the church was to be carried to "the uttermost parts," and this was to continue throughout the gospel age. When the church was launched, and through its first years, it was under the direction of men immediately guided by the Holy Spirit. These men must sometime die. It was necessary that they who were guided by the Holy Spirit should write down the teachings of Jesus and the facts of His life, death and resurrection for the guidance of men when the apostles had passed on.

Thus, as men should go forth to preach the gospel through the centuries to come they would have back of them the same truths that the inspired original founders had. The Gospels, as written, were an absolute essential to the spreading abroad of the church to all people in all lands through all time.

II. A Fuller Revelation of God

Jesus had many purposes in coming to earth. He said, "The Son of man is come to seek and to save that which was lost" (Luke 19:10). This could be said to be the chief and central purpose. He said, "I am come that they might have life, and that they might have it mor abundantly" (John 10:10). Among the many purposes of His coming was that we might know the Father. Those who had only the Scriptures of the Old Testament had but a hazy conception of God as a *Father,* a *heavenly Father,* a *loving heavenly Father.* Jesus talked continually about the Father. He came to get men really acquainted with God, with God's abounding love and mercy as well as His justice and power.

While Jesus was here on earth He could teach by word of mouth. He also provided for the giving of His teaching to the whole world for all time. In these Gospels we find the fuller revelation of a loving heavenly Father, the heavenly Head of the great family which makes up the church.

III. A REVELATION OF CHRIST, THE SAVIOUR

As facts stand today, the only possible approach to Christ, the only possible knowledge we may have of Him, of His teaching, of His way of life, is through the records in these four Gospels, written by real and living contemporary witnesses. Some men, who have but slight regard for the reliability of the Gospel records, talk of getting "back to Christ." It should be remembered that the only possible road back to Christ is through these Gospels of Matthew, Mark, Luke and John.

While it is not the part of this volume to enter into lengthy and abundant proofs that these Gospels record the inspired Word of God and that they came from one directing Mind who could have been none other than God, yet we call attention to the fact that such abundant proofs are not lacking.

These Gospel records reveal not only a historical character known as the Christ, but their whole intent and purpose is to reveal Him as the Saviour of mankind, the *Son of the living God*. Through these records alone may we come to know Him as such. This is indeed important to the church, His church, the New Testament church.

IV. A REVELATION OF BASIC TRUTHS

Not only do the Gospels reveal the Saviour, Christ, but they also reveal some basic truths about man and his life here and hereafter. These revealed truths are such that man could not discover them through his own wisdom or research. Following are samples of revealed truths which could not possibly be discovered through wisdom or research:

No man cometh unto the Father, but by me.—John 14: 6.

Not every one that saith unto me, Lord, Lord, shall enter into the kingdom of heaven; but he that doeth the will of my Father which is in heaven.—Matt. 7: 21.

There is therefore now no condemnation to them which are in Christ Jesus, who walk not after the flesh, but after the Spirit.—Rom. 8: 1.

For as many of you as have been baptized into Christ have put on Christ.—Gal. 3: 27.

I am the way, the truth, and the life.—John 14: 6.

These are truths which man unaided would be unable to discover, but which are revealed for us in the Gospels. To reveal means to "unveil" or "uncover" that which is hid. In the Gospels we discover not only what God has done to save us and what Jesus has done and will do, but we discover that there is something for *us* to do. These are but samples of the many truths of like kind revealed in the Gospels. These truths are absolutely essential and basic when we come to contemplate His church.

V. Books of Evidence of Christ's Deity

As we have formerly emphasized, the deity of Christ is the rock foundation of the church. The Gospels contain the evidence of His deity. While we frequently refer to the Gospels as "biographies" of Christ, this is not exactly true if we mean biographies in the ordinary sense of the word. None of them claim to give but a minute fraction of the facts of His life and teaching. None of them pretend to relate such facts as they give, in a chronological order. Rather than biographies they are books of evidences of His deity compiled by four contemporary witnesses. The purpose of evidence is to establish a truth. The truth to be established by those four witnesses is that Jesus is the Christ, the Son of the living God. Hence, each writer records his own testimony showing individuality, sincerity, truthfulness. Thus are the proofs substantiated by the testimony of four witnesses.

And many other signs truly did Jesus in the presence of His disciples, which are not written in this book: but these are written, that ye might believe that Jesus is the Christ, the Son of God; and that believing ye might have life through his name.—John 20: 30, 31.

VI. EVIDENCES OF THE DIVINE INSPIRATION OF THE ENTIRE BIBLE

The Gospels furnish an essential link in the evidences of the divine inspiration of the entire Bible. The Bible as the Word of God is essential to the church. Without it as a revelation from God the church would be hopelessly adrift. Not only do the Gospels reveal the Christ, but the very records themselves claim to be given by inspiration and contain evidence that they could not have been produced, as they were, otherwise. Then we may note that the perfect meshing of these Gospel records with the prophecies and promises recorded in the Old Testament through fifteen hundred preceding centuries furnishes one of the unanswerable evidences of the divine inspiration of the whole.

VII. THE GOSPELS PAVE THE WAY FOR THE FACTS RECORDED IN THE BOOK OF ACTS

While the Book of Acts records the history of the founding and first days of the church, yet Acts would be incomprehensible today but for the records contained in the Gospels. The Gospels reveal the Christ as Saviour, giving proofs of His deity and revealing what He did toward our salvation. They also reveal that there is something for us to do. The Gospels contain that which would lead us to desire to be Christians, but leave the question as to *how* to become Christians unanswered except in the most general terms. The Gospels reveal that there is something for us to do, but leaves us with the question,

"Lord, what wilt thou have me to do?" The Book of Acts follows logically to answer that question.

QUESTIONS

1. How were the apostles divinely guided and instructed in the first days of the church?

2. How are we divinely guided and given the same truths today?

3. In what respects do the Gospels reveal God more fully than the Old Testament?

4. From what source may we get our whole and only knowledge of Jesus today?

5. Aside from a historical knowledge of the historical Christ, what additional revelation of Jesus is in the Gospels?

6. Give a number of Scriptural revelations to be found in the Gospels regarding man's life here and hereafter.

7. Why is it necessary that these truths should be revealed?

8. What is the real purpose of the Gospels, biographical or evidential?

9. What is the one basic truth which they are written to establish?

10. What relation has this truth to the church?

11. In what ways do the Gospels help to demonstrate the divine inspiration of the whole Bible?

12. How do the Gospels pave the way for the ongoing of the church today?

Chapter V

Founding and Early History of the New Testament Church

I. THE BOOK OF ACTS

Just as the Old Testament and the Gospels contain the records of all the *preparations* for founding the church of Christ, the Book of Acts contains the record of its *founding, early growth and spread*. To know and recognize the church of the New Testament we must know the Book of Acts. The book serves two very definite and logical purposes. It is not only the history of the founding of the church or kingdom on earth, but it is the book of examples of Holy-spirit-guided conversions. By this means it answers conclusively the question, "What shall I do to be saved?"

The author of the book is unquestionably Luke, who also wrote the Gospel of Luke prior to the writing of Acts. It was written about the year A. D. 63, within a very few years of the time of the writing of the three synoptic Gospels. It constitutes a logical sequel to the Gospels.

II. THE ESSENTIAL PURPOSE OF ACTS

1. An Answer to the Question, "What Shall I Do to Be Saved?"—The Book of Acts takes up where the Gospels leave off. In the Gospels we learn what *Jesus* did and taught. In the Gospels we also learn that there are some things for us to do.

Not every one that saith unto me, Lord, Lord, shall enter into the kingdom of heaven; but he that doeth the will of my Father which is in heaven.—Matt. 7:21.

The Book of Acts answers the question, What shall I do? The Gospels prepare us to *want to become* Christians, the Book of Acts tells us *how to become* Christians.

2. A Completion and Fulfillment of Things Prepared for in the Gospels.—Again we may recall that in the Gospels Jesus tells the apostles to go to Jerusalem and tarry until they should be endued with power from on high (Luke 24:49). In Acts we are told of their obedience to this command and the fulfillment of this promise (Acts 2:1-4). We also recall Jesus' promise to send the Holy Spirit, who should guide them into all truth and call to their remembrance all that He had said unto them (John 16:13; 14:26). In Acts we find the record of the fulfillment of this promise (Acts 2). Thus, these chosen men, endued and guided by the Holy Spirit whom Jesus sent, answered inquiring men as to exactly what to do to be saved (Acts 2:37-42). Here then is the essential purpose of the Book of Acts.

III. How the Question of What to Do to Be Saved Is Answered

The question as to what to do to become a Christian, a follower of Christ, a saved person is answered not only once, but a number of times. It is answered not only by one inspired person, but by a number. It is answered for people of many different conditions. The good, God-fearing, praying Lydia (Acts 16:13-15, 40) is told what she must do. On the other hand, Paul, the bitterest of enemies of Christ and a persecutor of the church, is told what he must do (Acts 9:1-20). Cornelius, a foreigner and soldier, who was a near-perfect character, reverent and devout, was told what he must do (Acts 10). On Pentecost, Jews and proselytes of seventeen different nationalities and tongues were told what to do (Acts 2:7-11, 37, 38). Later, the jail keeper in Philippi, a Gentile wholly untaught, was told what to do (Acts 16:29-34). The Ethiopian eunuch was told what to do (Acts 8:35-40). Thus we have sample conversions in Acts which answer the question, What shall *I do?* Those who did not yet believe were first told to believe on the Lord, and were taught so that they might believe. Those who did believe were told to repent. Those who believed and showed evidence of sincere repentance were told to be baptized. The answers varied according to the state of progress of the inquirer.

IV. A Summary of the New Testament Procedures

A summary as shown in these divinely given samples of conversion shows the following procedures:

1. The gospel preached (Acts 2:14ff; Acts 8:35).
2. Believed or received the Word (Acts 4:4; 18:8; 2:41).
3. Repented of their sins (Acts 2:38; 16:32-34).
4. Confessed their faith in Christ (Acts 8:37).
5. Baptized into Christ in the name of the Father, Son and Holy Spirit (Acts 2:38 or any of the conversions cited).
6. Continued steadfastly in the apostles' doctrine, fellowship, breaking of bread and prayers (Acts 2:42); ministered to the saints (2 Cor. 9:1); gave generously (Acts 4:32-35); went everywhere preaching the Word (Acts 8:4).

V. How the Church Came to Be

The beginning or birth of the church was on Pentecost, fifty days after the resurrection or ten days after the ascension. The procedure as learned from this and the other instances was as follows:

1. Peter preached the gospel of Christ according to the commission given by Christ as recorded in Matt. 28:18-20.
2. The people believed the facts about Christ.
3. They repented of their sins against Christ.
4. They were baptized into Christ (Gal. 3:27).

5. They were thus added to the list of the saved, i. e., to the group of those who are "in Christ."
6. The Lord added to them, to the church, daily such as were saved (Acts 2:47).
7. They continued steadfastly (Acts 2:42).
8. Three thousand were thus added on this first day (Acts 2:41).
9. Soon the number of men was five thousand (Acts 4:4).
10. Soon both men and women in large numbers and also a great number of Jewish priests were added (Acts 5:14; 6:7).
11. They that were scattered abroad went everywhere preaching the Word (Acts 8:4).
12. Philip carried the work to Samaria (Acts 8:5, 6).
13. The Ethiopian carried the message to Africa (Acts 8:26-40).
14. Peter carried the work to Cæsarea and the west coast (Acts 10).
15. Men of Cyprus taught the way in Antioch of Syria, where the disciples first began to be called "Christians" (Acts 11:19-21, 26).
16. Ananias, Saul and others proclaimed the message in Damascus (Acts 9:20-22).
17. Paul and his helpers spread the teaching throughout western Asia, and he with others carried it to Europe (Acts 13ff).
18. By this time the churches had come to be known as "churches of Christ," "church of God," "church of the living God" (Acts 20:28; Rom. 16:16; 1 Tim. 3:15).

VI. SUPPLEMENTAL HISTORY AND INSTRUCTIONS

While the Book of Acts tells of the founding of the church and its earliest history, there is much added in a supplemental way in the Epistles and somewhat in the Book of Revelation.

In these books we learn more of the persecutions and of the false teachers and teachings that sprang up as the church spread. We get a more intimate view of quite a number of these churches that were planted. We get additional hints that throw added and confirming light on the processes of conversion and reasons for becoming Christians. Examples are found in Rom. 6:3, 4, and Col. 2:12. We learn of the blessings and promises to the faithful, and of the penalties and punishments for the individuals that were unfaithful.

1. Reasons for becoming Christians (Rom. 6:22, 23).
2. Reasons for being baptized (Rom. 6:3, 4; Gal. 3:27; Rom. 8:1).
3. False teachers (2 Pet. 2:1-3).
4. Fate of the faithful and the unfaithful (Revelation 1, 2, 3).

QUESTIONS

1. In what book do we find the history of the birth and early days of the church?

2. What two main purposes does the Book of Acts serve?

3. Who is the author of Acts, and what other book of the Bible did he write?

4. What important question that is asked in the Gospels is definitely answered in Acts?

5. What Gospel promises find their fulfillment in Acts?

6. Why can the Gospel answers given by Peter, Paul and the rest be counted as God's answers?

7. What method is used in Acts to answer the question, "What must I do to be saved?"

8. How does one account for the answers not always being the same.

9. Summarize the complete series of procedures as gathered from all the answers.

10. Give a running summary of the beginning and early spread of the church.

11. What name was soon applied to the members of the church?

12. What names were used for the church?

13. How do the Epistles and Revelation supplement the history as given in Acts?

Chapter VI

The Gospel Plan as Applied to the Church

I. GOD IS A GOD OF ORDER AND PLAN

The gospel is the outcome and consummation of a plan which is noticeable throughout the Old Testament and the Gospels. God is the great Planner. One who studies any department of science, whether it be botany, chemistry, bacteriology, astronomy, physiology or any other, can not help but note and be impressed by the plan, design and order everywhere evident. God is the designer of all this order.

In the saving of man, God did not depart from His orderly and planned procedure. There is definite and clear plan to which man is asked to accommodate himself if he would reap the blessings which God provides. Not only is this true throughout all the physical realm, but is likewise true in the spiritual realm. Man can not defy nor disregard God's plan in nature and live. Neither can he in the spiritual realm. Thus is it necessary for the plan of salvation to be revealed. This is done in the New Testament Scriptures. It must be a plan which man can understand, and it must be one to which it is possible for man to conform.

II. REQUISITES OF A PLAN WHICH CONFORMS TO MAN AS HE IS

God made man in His own image. This means that he is a sentient, a reasoning, a thinking being with the power to consider, decide, choose and act. When man considers he must have facts to consider. Man, as God made him, weighs facts, exercises his reasoning powers, chooses that which God-given

31

reason indicates as the true, the worth-while, the best, the right. Then man acts upon these conclusions. In psychology, these powers and processes are classified as intellect, sensibility and will.

A plan which God makes for man's salvation and in which co-operative action is called for must fit the man whom God has made. Such a plan would call for:

1. Facts and truths with evidence to substantiate them.
2. These facts and truths made available to man.
3. A hearing of these facts with their proofs.
4. Believing the facts.
5. A choice of action or conclusion.
6. Action upon the conclusion.

III. THE PLAN AS REVEALED

The plan of salvation, when summarized, reveals that we are saved through Christ, redeemed by Christ, come to God only through Christ. It is indicated that ''faith'' (whole-hearted belief) in Christ is a positive requisite. ''Without faith it is impossible to please him: for he that cometh to God must believe that he is, and that he is a rewarder of them that diligently seek him'' (Heb. 11: 6). Obedience is also indicated clearly. ''Not every one that saith unto me, Lord, Lord, shall enter into the kingdom of heaven; but he that doeth the will of my Father which is in heaven'' (Matt. 7: 21). ''Repent, and be baptized every one of you in the name of Jesus Christ for the remission of sins, and ye shall receive the gift of the Holy Ghost'' (Acts 2: 38).

Is there an order in these processes that fits man as God made him? The Scriptures reveal such an orderly plan, and it has been called, ''The *plan* of salvation.'' It presents:

1. Facts, Evidence, Proofs.—We are to believe in Christ, but first we are presented with abundant and logical proofs that He is the Christ, the Son of the living God. A Christ is presented who gave *perfect* teaching, who lived perfectly His perfect teaching, One in whom no man then or since has been able to find one flaw. It is in this Christ that man is asked to believe. The Old Testament and the Gospels furnish the proofs of His being the Son of the living God.

2. Faith in Christ.—Faith is required only after the facts and evidence have been presented. Here God employs man's intellect, his knowing, thinking, reasoning powers. Hence, so far God's plan fits God's man.

3. Repentance.—In repentance the sensibilities are employed. Remorse, sorrow, appreciation, feeling and love come into play.

4. Confession of Faith.—Often man's actions are strengthened and hastened by an open declaration of intent to act. Confession of faith in Christ "with the mouth" before men is in one sense such an act or declaration.

5. Baptism.—Baptism is a physical act with a spiritual purpose and significance. It is an open act of obedience subject to the action of man's will and choice.

6. Growth in Grace and Knowledge of the Truth.—Growth in grace and knowledge of the truth is the natural outcome of the new direction of life and purpose of life as determined by the foregoing steps.

Thus the Scripturally designated *plan* of salvation follows logically and conforms perfectly to the logical reactions of God's man.

IV. THE PLAN SUMMARIZED AND SIMPLIFIED

1. Hearing the gospel of Christ.
   "Faith cometh by hearing" (Rom. 10:17).
2. Believing the gospel evidence about Christ.
   "Without faith it is impossible to please him" (Heb. 11:6).
3. Repentance of sin and of disobedience to Christ.

"Now commandeth all men every where to repent" (Acts 17:30).

4. Confession of faith in Christ.
   "With the heart man believeth unto righteousness; and with the mouth confession is made unto salvation" (Rom. 10:10).

5. Baptism into Christ.
   "As many of you as have been baptized into Christ have put on Christ" (Gal. 3:27).

6. Wearing the name of Christ.
   "The disciples were called Christians" (Acts 11:26).

7. Growing spiritually in Christ.
   "Grow in grace, and in knowledge" (2 Pet 3:18).

8. Persevering in service to Christ in His church.
   "Be thou faithful unto death" (Rev. 2:10).

9. Heir of all the blessings and promises of Christ.
   "I will give thee a crown of life" (Rev. 2:10).

As each of these phases of the gospel plan will receive treatment in detail in later chapters, we merely list them here in their Scriptural and logical order. The one thought to be gained in this lesson is that *there is* a definite *gospel plan,* and that it is logically presented in the Scriptures as here summarized. We gain a deeper understanding of the significance and importance of each element of the plan as we study each in detail as presented in the Scriptures.

V. ADVANTAGES OF THE GOSPEL PLAN

The unsaved of the world are confused by the multiplicity of plans of salvation by which they are confronted. Some turn away in despair, some repudiate the gospel itself because its beautiful and logical simplicity has been obscured by the multiplied and differing plans offered. There are a number of advantages in the gospel plan.

1. The very fact that the gospel is a *divinely* given plan marks its first advantage.
2. That it proposes a sane, logical and practical procedure is a second advantage.
3. Its very simplicity, "so that a wayfaring man, though a fool, need not err therein," is a positive advantage.
4. It adds nothing and leaves out nothing that the inspired Word calls for.
5. There is no contradiction in any of its parts, and no contradiction of the logical processes of the human heart.
6. It is eminently practical as well as wholly spiritual. It is a plan that any one can understand. It calls for things which any one can do and is such that any one can unfold it to another.

VI. How All This Is Related to the New Testament Church

In this lesson we have made a study of the "Gospel Plan of Salvation." That is, we have followed the New Testament to find what it teaches men to do to be saved. This is the question asked and answered in the Scriptures. The answer as to how all this is related to the church, however, is found in Acts 2: 37-47 and other Scriptures which show that when any group in any place heard the gospel, believed it and obeyed it, this same group constituted the church in that place. What they did to be saved was exactly the same as what they did to *become* Christians. The group of Christians or disciples of Christ in any community constituted the church in that community. To summarize, when men did what the inspired teachers and preachers told them to do to be saved, they did what made them a part of the group of the saved, i. e., Christians, automatically, and at the same time members of Christ's body, Christ's church. There is no Scriptural suggestion of anything more required for membership in His body, the church.

QUESTIONS

1. Show how God provides for order and plan in all things.

2. What three requisites must the plan of salvation show if it is to apply to man?

3. What are the psychological groupings of man's mental processes as God made him?

4. Show how a plan of salvation must conform to these mental processes.

5. Name the steps in the plan of salvation, and show how they fit and follow man's natural mental processes.

6. Name in order ten steps in the gospel plan.

7. Give six advantages of the gospel plan.

8. What disadvantages appear if the gospel plan is changed?

9. How does the gospel plan of salvation relate to the church?

Chapter VII

Faith and Its Place in the Church

I. WHAT FAITH IS

Before making a study of "faith" and its place in the New Testament church, it is well to have in mind a clear notion of what we mean by faith.

1. Dictionary Definitions.—Webster's dictionary defines the word to mean: (a) "Belief in God, in revelation and such like"—"in a practical religious sense, trust in God." (b) "Fidelity to one's promises or allegiance to a deity, or to a person; loyalty." (c) "That which is believed; especially a system of religious belief."

2. Bible Definitions.—(a) "Faith is the assurance of things hoped for, a conviction (the proving) of things not seen" (Heb. 11:1, A.R.V.). (b) "Faith is the substance of things hoped for, the evidence of things not seen" (Heb. 11:1, A.V.).

3. A Summarized Definition.—From the above definitions and from other Scriptures on the subject of faith we give the following definition: "The unquestioned and unwavering [wholehearted] belief in God and in Christ based on evidence and testimony." Part of the substance of this definition comes from the Scripture statement, "So belief cometh of hearing, and hearing by the word of Christ" (Rom. 10:17, A.R.V.). "So then faith cometh by hearing, and hearing by the word of God" (Rom. 10:17, A.V.).

From these Scriptures we learn that faith and wholehearted belief are practically synonymous, and that faith (or belief) is a natural result of certain conditions.

37

II. Different Uses of the Word "Faith"

Before we proceed further, it is well to note that the word "faith" is used in three different senses in the New Testament, just as it is given three meanings in the dictionary. These three uses are:

1. A Wholehearted Belief in God or Christ or the Revealed Truth, Based on Evidence and Testimony.—Scriptural examples:

(a) Rom. 10: 17, cited above.
(b) "Though I have all faith," etc. (1 Cor. 13: 2).
(c) "We walk by faith, not by sight" (2 Cor. 5: 7).
(d) "Taking the shield of faith" (Eph. 6: 16).

2. The System of Christian Doctrine.—Scriptural examples of the use of the word might be:

(a) "For obedience to *the* faith" (Rom. 1: 5).
(b) "Fast in *the* faith" (1 Cor. 16: 13).
(c) "My own son in *the* faith" (1 Tim. 1: 2).

3. As Synonymous With "Faithfulness" or "Loyalty."—A Scriptural example would be:

"Your patience and faith in all your persecutions" (2 Thess. 1: 4).

This study is of faith as defined under paragraph (1) above, i. e., wholehearted belief in Jesus Christ as the Son of the living God and Saviour of men.

III. Necessity for and Importance of Faith

1. Faith an Absolute Requirement.—The New Testament Scriptures throughout make plain that faith in Christ is an absolute essential and requirement.

Without faith it is impossible to please him.—Heb. 11: 6.
Believe on the Lord Jesus Christ, and thou shalt be saved.—Acts. 16: 31.
God so loved the world, that he gave his only begotten Son, that who-

soever believeth in him should not perish, but have everlasting life.—John 3 : 16.

Thy faith hath made thee whole.—Matt. 9 : 22.

2. Faith Heads the List of Gospel Steps.—Faith stands at the head of the list of steps into the church, i. e., into Christ. The gospel plan of salvation, as we recall, listed (a) faith, (b) repentance, (c) confession, (d) baptism, (e) the life of service in and for Christ. This being a divine plan we can not hope or expect to be saved if we eliminate any portion of it, especially its very beginning.

3. Gospel Steps Rest on Faith.—The other steps depend on faith. Without faith, *repentance* would be impossible; *confession* would be a hypocrisy; *baptism* would be an empty form, meaningless and useless, and the *Christian life* would be stripped of all that makes it possible or desirable.

IV. THE ONE CENTER OF FAITH

There are many faiths. Even today an impression seems to persist that it makes little difference what or in whom we believe so long as we believe sincerely. A study of the faith that obtained as a feature of the New Testament church was a faith *in Christ* to the exclusion of all other faiths. Jesus, Peter, Paul and John all teach pronouncedly that the only saving or acceptable faith is faith in Christ as the Son of God. There was no room for faith in Baal or in sorcery, in the isms of the philosophers, yea, not even in Paul, Peter or Apollos. "Were ye baptized in the name of Paul?" (1 Cor. 1 : 13).

V. A VITAL, ACTIVE FAITH

The faith portrayed as a feature of the church of the New Testament was one that laid hold on life. In vain may we attempt or long to restore the *life* of the New Testament church unless the *faith* of the New Testament church be restored. Life was given a fixed and burning purpose; death was divested of its terrors. Sacrifice became a joy; service became a passion. Death became a fulfillment and the beginning of a crowned life.

VI. To Restore the New Testament Church and Its Life and Fruits

As said above, to restore the *New Testament church* calls for restoring the *New Testament life*. But to restore the New Testament *life* calls for a restoration of the New Testament *faith*. Since "faith cometh by hearing," it is evident that to restore *New Testament faith* calls for a restoration of *New Testament preaching*.

New Testament preaching was vital. It was done with conviction, it produced conviction. It never got away from the Christhood of Christ, the authority of Christ, the commands of Christ, loyalty to Christ, service in Christ and the rewards of Christ. Mere space-filling oratory on themes calculated to tickle the ears had no place in the preaching of the New Testament church. True, there were theorists, philosophizers, Judaizers, "ism" promoters, and such like, but these the New Testament frowned upon and controverted most pronouncedly. Christ was preached as the Son of God, Redeemer, Saviour and, finally, as Judge.

VII. A Wholehearted Faith

The faith commanded and commended in the New Testament is belief with the *whole heart*. In the New Testament the word *heart* is very frequently used as synonymous with *mind*. Let us remember that the human mind includes *intellect, sensibilities* (feelings, passions, etc.) and *will*. A faith which touches or involves only the intellect is one which involves but one-third of the heart. Mere intellectual assent to the facts presented is not the faith called for. New Testament faith or belief calls not only for intellectual conviction, but for the love and loyalty of the emotional powers of the heart and for the action of the will. A faith which stops short of love and obedience is not the New Testament faith. In the light of this truth it becomes apparent that John 3:16 in no sense contradicts Acts 2:38 or Luke 13:3.

For God so loved the world, that he gave his only begotten Son, that whosoever believeth in him should not perish, but have everlasting life.— John 3:16.

Then Peter said unto them, Repent, and be baptized every one of you in the name of Jesus Christ for the remission of sins, and ye shall receive the gift of the Holy Ghost.—Acts 2:38.

I tell you, Nay: but, except ye repent, ye shall all likewise perish.— Luke 13:3.

As important as faith is, and though it is an absolute requirement, it is yet evident that "faith alone" is not sufficient. It is the first step but not the last. Unless fulfilled by obedience, love, loyalty and service it becomes "dead, being alone," and is, therefore, not the faith which the New Testament calls for and God requires.

QUESTIONS

1. Give a clear definition of faith.

2. Give a synonym of Bible faith.

3. In what three senses is the word "faith" used in the New Testament? Give Scriptural illustrations.

4. Give a Scriptural quotation showing faith to be a positive essential.

5. Give the gospel plan of salvation, showing where faith stands in relation to other steps.

6. If faith is absent, what effect does it have on the other steps?

7. What is the center of New Testament faith, or in whom does New Testament faith center?

8. Does it leave room for other faiths?

9. What constitutes the basis for faith in Christ?

10. What are some of the characteristics of this faith?

11. What effect does a real and vital faith in Christ have on life?

12. To restore the New Testament life, what other restorations are called for and in what order?

13. Distinguish between mere intellectual belief and wholehearted faith or belief.

14. Show then how John 3:16 is not inconsistent with Acts 2:38 or Luke 13:3.

Chapter VIII

Repentance as Taught and Practiced in the New Testament Church

I. MEANING OF REPENTANCE

1. What the Word "Repentance" Means.—The word "repentance" comes from a Latin word which was translated from a Greek word. The Greek word, according to Milligan, meant "to change the mind." It is necessary to understand clearly what is meant by repentance and what is involved in it in order to understand clearly the New Testament teaching on the subject.

2. What Repentance Implies.—The word implies a turning, a complete reversal of direction and, being a mental or heart action, means a reversal of the mind or heart. This involves attitude and purpose. Being a mental change, a mind change, a heart change, it is something that can take place instantly. At the same time it is something that any one can do. That is, it is a voluntary act. God *commands repentance* for *all,* and God never commands impossibilities.

3. Necessary Prerequisites and Consequents to Repentance.—There are conditions and processes which precede repentance and which may take time, such as hearing, weighing the evidence and arriving at a conclusion. Likewise, there are consequents which follow repentance, such as confession of faith, baptism, building of Christian character to replace the sinful tendencies of life, and growth in grace and knowledge of the truth. These likewise take time. Repentance stands in between, is a mental or inward decision, it is a change of mind or heart that lends itself to "now" and, as said above, involves a change of attitude and purpose and, therefore, a change of the whole direction of life. Reversal of purpose must precede reversal of direction.

II. MEANING OF REPENTANCE AS USED IN THE NEW TESTAMENT

Repentance, as one of the steps in the gospel plan of salvation, has to do with decision as to *Christ*. There might be many repentances or reversals of purpose, attitude or plan in life, but here we study it only as it applies to Christ and one's attitude toward *Him*. It is repentance *toward Christ* that constitutes one of the steps in the New Testament plan of salvation. Christ only can save. Turning to walk with Him leads to salvation.

III. MISTAKEN NOTIONS ABOUT REPENTANCE

1. Repentance and Reform of Life.—Some think they can not repent, because they look upon repentance as the complete task of reform of life. They refuse, neglect or defer acceptance of Christ and obedience to Him because they do not feel capable of completely reforming their lives. They look upon repentance as "a getting rid of sin," by their own strength and resolution, as a preparation for accepting Christ. The repentance taught in the New Testament is a *decision to accept Christ and to follow Him* as the means for getting rid of sin.

2. Repentance and Sorrow.—Others forget that hearing of the Word and its resulting faith in God, in the Word of God and in Christ are the Bible preliminaries to repentance toward Christ. Knowledge of the Word and faith logically lead to a recognition of sin and to sorrow for it, but this is not yet repentance and should not be confused with it. This is what is Scripturally called, "Godly sorrow, leading to repentance." Following Godly sorrow comes the *decision* to reverse the former attitude toward Christ and to begin building a life in accord with His commands and His teaching. This is New Testament repentance.

IV. Repentance Illustrated

1. Repentance Is an "About Face."—Let us remember that repentance is a reversal, i. e., an *about face* as to Christ, a turning about from what we now recognize as wrong to that which we now recognize as right. It is not right to continue *to reject* Christ as the Saviour sent of God, so we "about face" in our decision to accept Him. It is not right to keep on saying "No" to His calls, therefore, we "about face" and say "Yes." It is wrong not to obey Christ, so we determine to "about face" and obey Him. We have not treated the Son of God well and that is sin. We decide, determine to accept, obey and serve Him. That is repentance toward Christ, and is the repentance commanded in the New Testament as a step in the plan of salvation.

2. Repentance Is an Inward Decision.—Repentance is thus an inward *decision* to change, to act upon something that up to this time we have not acted upon, to say "Yes" to something to which we have been saying "No," to go forward whereas we have been holding back.

3. Repentance Toward Christ.—One might be sincerely sorry for having mistreated (sinned against) a neighbor. One might truly repent and do works meet for repentance toward the neighbor, but this would not be the repentance required. We repeat, it is repentance *toward Christ* that is called for. When we truly repent toward Christ, however, we automatically repent toward all others.

V. Universal Need for Repentance

The New Testament Scriptures make plain that "repentance" is something that applies to *all*.

For *all* have sinned, and come short of the glory of God.—Rom. 3: 23.
I tell you, Nay: but, except ye repent, ye shall *all* likewise perish.—Luke 13: 3.

The times of ignorance therefore God overlooked; but now he commandeth men that they should *all everywhere repent.*—Acts 17: 30, A.R.V.

Repent, and be baptized *every one of you* in the name of Jesus Christ for the remission of sins.—Acts 2: 38.

Repent and turn to God.—Acts 26: 20.

Jesus saith unto him, I am the way, the truth, and the life: no man cometh unto the Father, but by me.—John 14: 6.

From the above Scriptures it becomes plain that there are *no* exceptions. *All* have sinned. The gospel is for *all*. *All* are *commanded* to repent. Note that God "commandeth" and that no man can come to the Father save through Christ. God commands *all* to repent. God never commands men to do what they can not do. Therefore, not only *all* are *commanded* to repent, but *all* can repent. From the foregoing study of repentance it becomes plain that, as taught and commanded in the New Testament church, repentance is something that *all* can do *now*.

VI. THE PLACE OF REPENTANCE IN THE GOSPEL PLAN

The nature of repentance logically determines its place and position in the New Testament plan of salvation. Repentance toward Christ could not possibly precede a knowledge of Christ which leads to faith in Him as the Son of God. On the other hand, surrender to Christ's will, such as takes place in the decision of repentance, naturally precedes the first open act of obedience which is "confession of faith in Christ," "with the mouth," "before men." Certainly, repentance must precede baptism, else baptism would be robbed of its major significance as a consummating act of obedience to Christ and an induction "into Christ." Thus the order as it appears in the conversions recorded in the New Testament follows logically the natural reactions and processes of the heart of man, i. e., to hear, to believe, to choose or decide, then to act upon that decision. Thus God's plan is not only fitted to man as God made him, but is beautiful in its simplicity.

VII. Repentance and Conversion

Lest it should be felt that an important matter has been consciously omitted, we add this final paragraph. Theologians have made much of the term "conversion," and in their arguments as to what it constitutes and how it is brought about have generated much heat and little light.

Conversion is a perfectly good New Testament term. What does it mean? Is it synonymous with "repentance," does it include more or is it something entirely different?

The noun "conversion" occurs once in the New Testament (Acts 15:3). "The conversion of the Gentiles" refers evidently to the fact that these Gentiles had "heard the Word," "believed the Word," "repented" and "been baptized into Christ." That is, they were added to the Lord and had been formed into churches. This is the report made to the brethren by Paul and Barnabas, and evidently refers to the whole and complete process by which these brethren became Christians. The verb "convert" or "converteth" occurs twice (Jas. 5:19, 20): "He which converteth the sinner from the error of his way shall save a soul from death," etc. Quite evidently this refers to the whole process of salvation as above.

The passive form "be converted" occurs six times in the King James Version, but in the Revised Version it does not appear at all (Matt. 13:15; Mark 4:12; Luke 22:32; John 12:40; Acts 3:19; Acts 28:27). It is there translated "turn ye" or "turned again." The King James reading is an admitted mistranslation of an active voice verb into the passive voice. The Revised Version gives the correct translation, and in these cases the term could be synonymous with "repent" or could comprehend the whole and completed process of becoming a Christian. There is, therefore, no need of confusion or argument over the term "conversion" if we understand the Scriptural meaning of repentance and know the New Testament plan of salvation.

QUESTIONS

1. What is the basic meaning of the word ''repent''?

2. What is implied in the meaning of the word?

3. Is repentance a voluntary act?

4. What conditions precede and what follows repentance?

5. Distinguish between repentance toward Christ and repentance toward others. Which is meant in the Bible command to repent?

6. In what respect is repentance frequently misapprehended?

7. Illustrate what is actually involved in Bible repentance.

8. Since according to our standards all are not equally guilty, why do *all* need to repent?

9. Quote Scriptures showing the universal need for repentance.

10. Show the logical place of repentance in the gospel plan.

11. What is the relation of repentance to conversion?

Answer. Conversion as used in the Scriptures implies the entire operation involved in becoming a Christian, repentance is one of the steps in the process.

Chapter IX

Confession of Faith in Christ

I. Nature of the New Testament Church Confession

In the attempts that have been made to simplify and clarify the steps in the gospel plan of salvation, this step has been designated by the one word, "confession." This has tended to obscure the tremendous truth underlying that which is designated in the New Testament as "the good confession." To get at the full import of the step, it is important to have its full New Testament description. It is not mere confession, but "confession of 'faith' in Christ"—"with the mouth"— "before men." That is the confession which is a definite step in and an integral part of the gospel plan. If Christ be eliminated from it, its whole significance is lost. The following Scriptures will give a clear picture of "the good confession":

And Simon Peter answered and said, Thou art the Christ, the Son of the living God.—Matt. 16: 16.
And Philip said, If thou believest with all thine heart, thou mayest. And he answered and said, I believe that Jesus Christ is the Son of God.—Acts 8: 37.
Whosoever shall confess that Jesus is the Son of God, God dwelleth in him, and he in God.—1 John 4: 15.
For with the heart man believeth unto righteousness; and with the mouth confession is made unto salvation.—Rom. 10: 10.
Whosoever therefore shall confess me before men, him will I confess also before my Father which is in heaven.—Matt. 10: 32.

II. Importance of the Good Confession

So much has been said and written about "faith," "repentance" and "baptism" that it has tended to make it appear

48

that the good confession is of little or minor importance. No one of these steps is important as only a ritualistic performance. It is not the mere making of the confession that counts, but that which it comprehends and signifies.

1. The Good Confession Is a Definite Part of the Divine Plan or Gospel Plan.—As we study the church of the New Testament, it becomes evident that the public confession that Jesus is the Christ was a definite procedure. It is said of Christ that, before Pilate, He witnessed "the good confession" (1 Tim. 6 : 13). It is said of Timothy that he "did confess the good confession before many witnesses" (1 Tim. 6 : 12, A.R.V.). All Christians are exhorted to hold fast "our confession" (Heb. 4 : 14, A.R.V.). In Heb. 10 : 23, A.R.V., it is called "the confession." To quote Robert Milligan: "From such expressions, then, it is very manifest that, in the apostolic church, a particular truth, most likely expressed in a given formula of words, was publicly confessed by all candidates for church membership . . . it was commonly known and designated as 'the good confession.' "

2. It Is a Statement of the Basic and Foundational Principle on Which the Whole Church Rests.—When Peter, on the trip to Cæsarea Philippi, made the confession, "Thou art the Christ, the Son of the living God," Jesus replied and said, "Upon this rock will I build my church" (Matt. 16 : 16, 18). Here is revealed the fundamental truth on which all the claims of Christianity rest and on which the church rests. A statement and a confession of faith in this fundamental truth is a most logical step for one becoming a Christian and a member of Christ's church.

III. THE PLACE OF THE GOOD CONFESSION IN THE NEW TESTAMENT CHURCH

From the Scriptures cited, it becomes evident that Jesus planned that those who accepted Him as Lord and Saviour should make that confession with their mouths before men; and that such was the practice in the early church.

While it is true that in the recorded conversions in Acts, the place and order of faith, repentance and baptism are mentioned many times and the good confession but once, and that in a verse which many scholars, including Alexander Campbell, have questioned, yet, if it is established that the making of the good confession was a definite procedure, it certainly had to have a place. The verse referred to (Acts 8:37) indicates that place which it occupied in the very early church, at least.*

It is also true that the nature of the good confession indicates its logical place. Such a confession could not be sincerely made preceding faith, it naturally would not be made prior to repentance or decision to accept and obey Christ. Baptism being the consummating step in gospel obedience would naturally follow confession. Thus its logical place is indicated as shown in Acts 8:37.

IV. SIGNIFICANCE OF THE GOOD CONFESSION

1. An Open Step Toward Christ.—Faith or believing is an inward matter. One may believe silently within the recesses of one's heart. Repentance is again an inward action of the human heart. Silently one repents or decides to yield to Christ's call, accept His way and obey His commands. In the gospel plan, however, God asks for some things in the open before God and man. Confession of faith in Christ with the mouth before men is the first such open step.

2. A Test of Faith and Repentance.—Confession being an outward or open step before men, it becomes a test of faith. While there is but one faith, faith in Christ, yet faith may have varying degrees of strength. It is capable of growth. Like any-

---

* This verse is not in some of the oldest manuscripts, but is in others which are very old, reaching back to the second century.

thing else, it must exercise or die. Confession is faith's first attempt to walk, and thus it begins to gain strength.

3. A Test of Courage.—Virtue, valor, courage are Christian virtues to be attained and cultivated. The open confession is a test of courage.

4. A Test of Purpose.—In repentance one purposes to obey and follow Christ. To confess faith before men is a first test of that newborn purpose. With the test, purpose grows stronger.

5. A Preparation for Future Growth in Christ.—A newborn Christian is called "a babe in Christ." There is much to follow—food, exercise and growth in grace and knowledge of the truth. This first open step of obedience constitutes a preparation for future obedience to Christ.

6. An Act With a Promise.—All Scripture consists of: *Facts* to be believed, *commands* to be obeyed, *promises* to be received by those who believe the facts and obey the commands and *warnings* to be heeded by all. Confession is an act which carries a definite promise. "Whosoever therefore shall confess me before men, him will I confess also before my Father which is in heaven" (Matt. 10: 32).

V. The Confession of Faith Stated

As the Scriptures plainly point out, the confession to be made is brief indeed. "Thou art the Christ, the Son of the living God." How can a statement so brief be of such consummate importance? The question answers itself when we analyze the Scriptural confession. It comprehends:

1. Belief in the *living God*.
2. Belief in *Christ* as *God's Son*.
3. Belief in *Christ* as *Saviour, Redeemer, Messiah* and *Lord*.
4. Faith in Christ as the *only* Saviour.
5. Belief in and acceptance of *Christ's Word* and *promises* as recorded in the New Testament.

6. Therefore, belief in the *Bible* as the *Word of God,* including both Old and New Testaments.
7. Belief in the *Holy Spirit* sent by Christ.
8. Belief in the *Word as given by the Holy Spirit.*
9. Belief in *life here and hereafter,* the *judgment,* heaven and hell as taught by Christ.
10. Acceptance of *Christ's way, Christ's plan* of salvation, *Christ's promises,* and *Christ's church* as our earthly place of service.

Thus this confession takes in everything that is divinely given and necessary and leaves out nothing that is divinely given and necessary. It is the good confession provided in God's wisdom and can not be improved upon by man's additions, subtractions or elaborations. It is the only confession Scripturally called for prior to baptism into Christ (Acts 8:37). Since it is thus all-inclusive of the whole ground of Christian faith, the fact stated in the good confession is frequently called "the creed of the church."

QUESTIONS

1. From what source can we gain the best and true understanding of the import and importance of "the good confession"?
2. Quote Scriptures showing what the confession is, what it includes and how it should be made.
3. Give two fundamental points which indicate the importance of "the good confession."
4. Give Scriptures indicating that the confession was a regular procedure in the apostolic church.
5. What is the basic truth on which the church and all the claims of Christianity rest?
6. How determine the place which the confession should have in the gospel plan.
7. Give six facts about the confession which show its purposes.
8. Quote the good confession as given by Peter, and show that it includes everything essential to Christian faith.

Chapter X

Baptism and the Church

I. BAPTISM, AND BAPTISM INTO CHRIST

Just as faith, to be of any avail in the saving of the soul, must be *faith in Christ;* just as repentance, to be of avail, must be *repentance toward Christ;* just as confession, to be of avail, must be sincere *confession of faith in Christ,* so must baptism be a *baptism into Christ,* if it is to be a New Testament baptism unto the remission of sins. There could be baptisms, many of which would have no relation to nor be any part of the divinely given plan of salvation. What are those necessary elements or conditions that make a baptism *a baptism into Christ* or make it *Christian baptism?* It is the purpose of this chapter to make a study of that question.

For as many of you as have been *baptized into Christ* have put on Christ.—Gal. 3 : 27.

Know ye not, that so many of us as were baptized into Jesus Christ were baptized into his death?—Rom. 6 : 3.

II. VARIOUS NEW TESTAMENT BAPTISMS

In order that "baptism into Christ" or "Christian baptism" may not be confused with other baptisms mentioned in the New Testament, it is well to have all these before us. They are:

1. John's Baptism.—While the actual act was the same, a burial in water, yet the purpose and significance were different. John's baptism was a baptism *unto repentance,* not *into Christ.* John's was a preparatory rite, significant of a cleansing in preparation for the coming Messiah.

2. The Baptism of Jesus.—While Jesus came to John and was baptized by him in Jordan, the purpose could not have been the same as the other baptisms by John. This baptism stood alone in purpose. The actual act was the same, but the purpose was "to fulfil all righteousness." Outside of this statement of Jesus we do not know the purpose. Jesus and God understood, and that was sufficient.

3. Baptism of the Holy Spirit.—(Acts 1:3-5; 2:1-4; Matt. 3:11.) This was a baptism which was to be administered *by* the Lord God Himself. It is not the baptism which Jesus authorized His followers to administer. The baptism of the Holy Spirit carried with it miraculous powers and was closely related to the impartation of inspired guidance. This was promised and given to chosen men, and was to obtain until the church should be established and the New Testament Word written, finished and closed. When this was accomplished there was no need for this special and inspired guidance, since the Holy Spirit could guide and instruct through His written Word from thence on.

4. Baptism Into Christ Unto (or for) the Remission of Sins.—This is the baptism which Jesus commanded His followers to administer, and the only one of the four that continues to this day and is to continue for all time. It is the baptism studied in this chapter (Matt. 28:18-20; Acts 2:38). Certainly it is made plain (Acts 2:38) that this baptism had the accompanying promise of "the gift of the Holy Spirit" which was a general promise to all and sundry who accepted and obeyed the Saviour.

III. AUTHORITY FOR CHRISTIAN BAPTISM

Baptism is a positive ordinance. It has no foundation in nature. It depends wholly on the expressed will and command of God. It is not something that man could arrive at by reason or logic, but rests wholly on the expression of divine will and instruction. Authority for it and for its place in the gospel plan of salvation must rest and does rest on divine command and instruction. When this is determined there is nothing left to be determined by human thought or reason but to obey. Scriptural authority for baptism is found not only in the direct Word of Jesus, but in the Word of the Holy Spirit as given through divinely guided (inspired) men.

All authority hath been given unto me in heaven and on earth. Go ye therefore, and make disciples of all the nations, baptizing them into the name of the Father and of the Son and of the Holy Spirit.—Matt. 28: 18, 19, A.R.V.

And he said unto them, Go ye into all the world, and preach the gospel to every creature. He that believeth and is baptized shall be saved; but he that believeth not shall be damned.—Mark 16: 15, 16.

The Holy Spirit speaking through Peter, the apostle, says:

Repent ye, and be baptized every one of you in the name of Jesus Christ unto the remission of your sins; and ye shall receive the gift of the Holy Spirit.—Acts 2: 38, A.R.V.

IV. WHAT BAPTISM IS AS DETERMINED FROM THE NEW TESTAMENT

There is and has been discussion and division as to what constitutes Christian baptism. This difference dates back to the Catholic Council of Ravenna, 1311. At that Council the assembled bishops voted to adopt sprinkling rather than immersion for the Roman Catholic Church on the theory that it was more convenient and that the church had the right and authority to make the change. The practice had crept in nearly five hundred years before, but this was its first official recognition. Many groups, as reforms branching from Catholicism, have continued the practice. The point of this paragraph is to determine what the Scriptures teach. It is not our purpose to present in this study arguments for affusion or to refute them. Neither shall we here attempt to present any part of the innumerable statements of church historians, leading scholars of all groups, Catholic and Protestant, and the definitions of the word as given in all Greek dictionaries. We believe the New Testament itself presents the matter so clearly that nothing more should be needed. The following is the New Testament Scriptures' description of each step, with the accompanying Scripture quotation:

1. The New Testament Plainly Describes the Act in Detail.

(a) Baptized *where there was much water.*

(a') And John also was baptizing in Ænon near to Salim, because there was much water there.—John 3: 23.

(b) They *came to the water.*

(b') And as they went on their way, they came unto a certain water: and the eunuch said, See, here is water; what doth hinder me to be baptized?—Acts 8: 36.

(c) Baptized *in water.*

(c') I indeed baptize you *in* water.—Matt. 3: 11, A.R.V. (See also Mark 1: 8; John 1: 26, A.R.V.)

(d) *In* the *River Jordan.*

(d') And were baptized of him in Jordan, confessing their sins.—Matt. 3: 6.

(e) They (both baptized and baptizer) went *down into the water.*

(e') And he commanded the chariot to stand still: and they went down both into the water, both Philip and the eunuch; and he baptized him.—Acts 8: 38.

(f) The candidate was *buried in semblance of Christ's burial.*

(f') Therefore we are buried with him by baptism into death.—Rom. 6: 4.

(g) The candidate was *raised up in semblance of Christ's resurrection.*

(g') That like as Christ was raised up from the dead by the glory of the Father, even so we

also should walk in newness of
life.—Rom. 6: 4.

(g') Buried with him in baptism,
wherein also ye are risen with him
through the faith of the operation
of God, who hath raised him from
the dead.—Col. 2: 12.

(h) They came up straightway
out of the water.

(h') And Jesus, when he was
baptized, went up straightway out
of the water.—Matt. 3: 16.

(h') And when they were come up
out of the water, the Spirit of the
Lord caught away Philip, that the
eunuch saw him no more: and he
went on his way rejoicing.—Acts
8: 39.

**2. The Word Used by Jesus and the Inspired Writers
Makes the Matter Plain.**—The word used by Jesus and the
apostles was the Greek word *baptidzo.* All standard Greek dictionaries, of which there are nearly fifty, give the meaning of
this word as, "to immerse, to dip, to submerge, to plunge." No
one of them gives the meaning as to "sprinkle" or to "pour."
Had Jesus meant to sprinkle He would have used the word
rantidzo; had He meant to pour, He would have used the word
cheo; had He meant merely to use water, regardless of how
applied, He would have used the word *hundraino.* Thus the
word used fits exactly in its meaning with the minutely described details of the act as shown in the Scriptures above. We
refer the student to any Standard Greek Dictionary.

V. UNANIMITY OF WORLD SCHOLARSHIP

While this brief chapter will not lend itself to quotations
from the accepted scholars of all denominations, yet we can state
that scholarship is agreed as to the meaning of the word and
as to the act described in the New Testament and practiced in
the early church under the apostles and for some centuries after.

Their universal testimony is that the primitive practice was immersion. The point to be established here is, what was taught and practiced in the New Testament church?

Of these scholars we name a few: Dean Alford (Episcopal), Albert Barnes (Presbyterian), John Calvin (Reformed), Adam Clarke (Methodist), Conybeare and Howson (Episcopal), Philip Doddridge (Presbyterian), Matthew Henry (Presbyterian), Luther and Lange (Lutheran), John Wesley (Methodist), Cornelius A. Lapide (Roman Catholic) and a great host of others representing the great scholars of all sects. The summarized statements of all these recognized scholars is that the primitive practice in the church of the New Testament was unquestionably a burial of the body in water.

VI. The Design or Purpose in Baptism

If we understand the act or action of baptism, its design becomes all the clearer.

1. It is an act of obedience to a positive command of Christ.
2. It is designed to picture Christ's burial and resurrection.
3. It typifies our burial with Him "by baptism."
4. It signifies our death to sin, and our resurrection to the new life in Christ.
5. It signifies our entrance "into Christ," into "the body of Christ," into "the church of Christ."
6. It signifies the:

End of the Old Life	Entrance Into the New Life
a. Out of Christ.	a. In Christ.
b. Without promise.	b. With all promise.
c. Unforgiven.	c. Forgiven.
d. Out of the kingdom.	d. In the kingdom.
e. In disobedience.	e. In obedience.
f. In sin.	f. In service.
g. With death as the end and the grave as the goal.	g. With eternal life and heaven as the end and goal.

VII. Place of Baptism in the Gospel Plan

The act of Christian baptism, its design or purpose and its significance, all definitely indicate its place in the gospel plan. Like the confession, it is an open act before the world. It is a *consummating* act in coming into Christ. "As many as have been baptized into Christ have put on Christ." But we have already found that it is impossible to come into Christ, i. e., become a Christian, except we wholeheartedly believe in Him, put our trust in Him, sincerely repent of our sins toward Him and openly own Him by confessing our faith in Him. Baptism, if it is to be Christian baptism, must have these New Testament prerequisites, else it is a mere physical act devoid of any real spiritual significance, blessing or promise.

VIII. An Act With a Promise

When the command to be baptized is carried out, as so clearly delineated in God's Word, when it thus represents the consummating act of a sincere faith in Christ, a sincere repentance toward Christ, a sincere acceptance of Christ and a sincere act of personal obedience to Christ, it carries with it promises, precious and far-reaching.

Then Peter said unto them, Repent, and be baptized every one of you in the name of Jesus Christ for the remission of sins, and ye shall receive the gift of the Holy Ghost.—Acts 2: 38.

For as many of you as have been baptized into Christ have put on Christ.—Gal. 3: 27.

There is therefore now no condemnation to them which are in Christ Jesus, who walk not after the flesh, but after the Spirit.—Rom. 8: 1.

He that believeth and is baptized shall be saved.—Mark 16: 16.

And this is the promise that he hath promised us, even eternal life.—1 John 2: 25.

IX. Christian Baptism Is a Spiritual Act

Baptism alone, i. e., immersion alone, would be a mere physical act without efficacy or promise. When it is done as a humble and sincere act of obedience to Christ, preceded by the heart changes implied in a sincere faith, a sincere repentance and a sincere acknowledgment of Christ as Saviour and Lord, then baptism becomes *Christian* baptism and has the deepest spiritual significance. It consummates the new birth; it completes the acts of obedience on which the precious promises are based; it marks the full entrance "into Christ," and, therefore, into the body of Christ, which is the church. Old sins are washed away, and one is now entitled to wear Christ's name and is now assured of God's favorable answer to prayer. One now may rest assured, not only by hope, but by the definite promises of God.

QUESTIONS

1. Distinguish between baptism and baptism into Christ.

2. Name the four baptisms mentioned in the New Testament and distinguish between them.

3. Which one of the four did Christ command His followers to administer?

4. Where does the authority for Christian baptism rest? Quote at least two Scriptures on the subject.

5. Name in order the detailed steps in baptism as described by the Scriptures.

6. What is the meaning of the original word used by Jesus when He commanded baptism.

7. What can you say as to the unanimity of world scholarship on New Testament baptism?

8. Name some of these leading scholars.

9. What do we learn from the New Testament as to the design or purpose of baptism?

10. Name a number of things which baptism denotes.

11. How can we determine the place or order of baptism in the gospel plan of salvation?

12. What are some of the promises coupled with baptism?

13. How does the physical act of baptism become a deeply significant spiritual act?

Chapter XI

New Testament Worship

I. THE EARLY BEGINNING OF WORSHIP

Just as worship was a definite phase of Judaism, so was it a definite phase of Christianity. The New Testament gives us clear pictures of the worship of the Christians from the beginning and through the days when they were under the direct guidance of the apostles who were in turn guided by the Holy Spirit sent by Christ. As soon as the gospel terms of pardon were proclaimed and men accepted and obeyed, they began to assemble for worship. This is plain from the following:

> Then they that gladly received his word were baptized: and the same day there were added unto them about three thousand souls. And they continued stedfastly in the apostles' doctrine and fellowship, and in breaking of bread, and in prayers.—Acts 2: 41, 42.

II. THE BASIC ELEMENTS OF NEW TESTAMENT WORSHIP

Note that in the above description of the worship, *four* specific elements are named. They are:

1. The Apostles' Doctrine.—There are today many doctrines. Many of them are conflicting. A church which aspires to follow the New Testament will be most conscientious in seeing that the doctrine preached from the pulpit and taught in the Bible school is strictly in accord with the New Testament teaching, i. e., the teaching of Christ and the apostles. Inasmuch as this entire volume is intended to be a presentation of the "apostles' doctrine," we need not elaborate further here.

2. The Fellowship.—The fellowship consisted in their assembling together for mutual admonition, mutual service and mutual contributions for needy brethren and for the promotion of the gospel message.*

3. Breaking of Bread.—This apparently was a regular practice from the beginning.*

4. The Prayers.—From the beginning the Christians were a praying people, and prayer was one of the outstanding features of their worship.*

Thus we see that the main features of Christian worship were four, all simple, all centering in Christ.

III. ADDITIONAL FEATURES

1. New Testament References Indicate That Worship Included Singing. In Paul's Epistles we find:

> Speaking to yourselves in psalms and hymns and spiritual songs, singing and making melody in your heart to the Lord; giving thanks always for all things unto God and the Father in the name of our Lord Jesus Christ.— Eph. 5: 19, 20.

> Let the word of Christ dwell in you richly in all wisdom; teaching and admonishing one another in psalms and hymns and spiritual songs, singing with grace in your hearts to the Lord. And whatsoever ye do in word or deed, do all in the name of the Lord Jesus, giving thanks to God and the Father by him.—Col. 3: 16, 17.

Be it noted that here is definite apostolic suggestion of music as a feature of the worship, and it includes not only *psalms*, but also *hymns* and *spiritual songs*. There is *no* definite instruction as to *how* this singing is to be performed, whether as solos or in chorus, whether from memory or from books, whether accompanied by instruments or not accompanied by instruments. These are matters on which the New Testament is silent. It is true that the singing of the psalms in Jewish worship was accompanied by instruments. If the New Testament had specified that instrumental music was to be used, then it would be obligatory to use it. If it had prohibited the use of instruments, then it would be obligatory *not* to use them. The fact is that the

---

* Each of these subjects will be treated quite fully in later chapters.

New Testament is silent on the subject. It is left to the worshipers to determine in love and co-operation in each congregation, but no one is given the instruction or authority to enforce his or her preference on all the rest.

2. Features Which Were Temporary.—Aside from the features named above, there are at least two others which are mentioned. They are *prophesyings* and *speaking in tongues.* These were features which were the direct result of the imparting of the Holy Spirit by the imposition of the hands of the apostles, and ceased with the passing away of the last of those to whom the apostles thus communicated those powers. By that time, however, the church was established, the Word of the New Testament was fully written and the message of instruction and prophecy closed. Thus there was no further need for this miraculous phase. From that time on it would only have lent confusion. From that time on our sole guide for Christianity is to be the New Testament Scriptures:

Every scripture inspired of God is also profitable for teaching, for reproof, for correction, for instruction which is in righteousness: that the man of God may be complete, furnished completely unto every good work.—2 Tim. 3: 16, A.R.V.

Note that the *Scriptures completely* furnish *every man everything* that is necessary unto *every* good work. When we add to the above the final injunction of John in the very close of the last chapter of the last book of the New Testament, it becomes plain that from that time *on,* no word of prophecy and no teaching in unknown tongues is in order. The inspired Scriptures alone are to be the guide.

For I testify unto every man that heareth the words of the prophecy of this book, If any man shall add unto these things, God shall add unto him the plagues that are written in this book: and if any man shall take away from the words of the book of this prophecy, God shall take away his part out of the book of life, and out of the holy city, and from the things which are written in this book.—Rev. 22: 18, 19.

IV. Time of Worship: The Lord's Day

While there is no indication that the preaching and teaching of the apostles' doctrine or the fellowship or the prayers were to be confined to but one day of the week, yet there is definite indication that from the very beginning a particular day was set aside specifically for worship. In the New Testament this day is called the "Lord's day" or "the first day of the week." There is no positive command that this should be done, but there is abundant evidence, Scriptural and historical, that it was done under the sanction, guidance and co-operation of the apostles who were in turn guided by the Holy Spirit.

Quite apparently the apostles and many of the Christians did not hesitate to preach the gospel "in the temple or synagogues," on the Sabbath (seventh day). They preached whenever and wherever they could get a hearing. They all prayed daily, and there are indications that, at first, Christians in Jerusalem commemorated the Lord's death and suffering daily. As the church took shape, however, the assembling for the "communion" and "fellowship," accompanied by preaching, centered on the "first day of the week," "the Lord's day."

And upon the first day of the week, when the disciples came together to break bread, Paul preached unto them, ready to depart on the morrow; and continued his speech until midnight.—Acts 20: 7.

Now concerning the collection for the saints, as I have given order to the churches of Galatia, even so do ye. Upon the first day of the week let every one of you lay by him in store, as God hath prospered him, that there be no gatherings when I come.—1 Cor. 16: 1, 2.

V. Interesting Facts About the Sanctions of the First Day by Jesus and the Apostles

1. It was on the first day of the week that Jesus came forth from the grave.
2. It was on the first day of the week of His resurrection that He made at least four of His appearances.

3. It was on the first day of the week that He appeared to all His apostles.
4. It was on the first day of the week that the Holy Spirit was sent according to His promise.
5. It was on the first day of the week that the gospel terms of pardon were first proclaimed.
6. It was on the first day of the week the church was born.
7. It was on the first day of the week that Jesus ascended.
8. It was on the first day of the week that His disciples therefore met to break bread in remembrance of Him, and to have fellowship in support of His church.

VI. THE CHRISTIAN DAY OF WORSHIP DETERMINED FULLY BY NEW TESTAMENT SCRIPTURES

The facts as cited from the New Testament should be conclusive. However, there are conscientious people who have been confused. The following facts may help clear the confusion. The Fourth Commandment, "Remember the sabbath day to keep it holy," is one of the Ten Commandments and as such is a part of the "Mosaic law." Let it be remembered that we today live in:

1. The Christian dispensation; not in the Mosaic.
2. We live under the gospel; not under the law.
3. Under Christ; not under Moses.
4. Of the Ten Commandments, the essence of nine was reincorporated in the teachings of Christ in a strengthened form, but this one was not.
5. Contrasts of the two days:

THE SABBATH	THE LORD'S DAY
Seventh day.	First day.
Common name, Saturday.	Common name, Sunday.
Day of rest.	Day of Christian service and worship.
Jewish day.	Christian day.

Marked by rest.	Marked by communion.
Commemorates finished work of creation and also deliverance from bondage in Egypt.	Commemorates resurrection of Christ and our deliverance from the bondage of death.

Wherefore the law was our schoolmaster to bring us unto Christ, that we might be justified by faith. But after that faith is come, we are no longer under a schoolmaster.—Gal. 3: 24, 25.

Constantine's Law.—Did Constantine change the Sabbath from the seventh day to the first? The answer is, No. The first day of the week was established as the day of Christian assembly and worship two and a half centuries before Constantine became emperor. From the social and economic, or even some other standpoint, any state or nation may choose the first day of the week and enact laws making it a legal holiday. This has been done many times, but this has nothing whatever to do with its status in the Christian system and economy. It would be the Lord's Day anyhow, and is, nevertheless.

Constantine was the first to enact such laws giving the day national recognition and status. Some have thus been confused and supposed that the Sabbath was thus changed from the seventh day to the first by human enactment. This is not the fact at all. Constantine merely was the first to enact civil law in regard to the activities of the people on the Lord's Day. The same has been done by many of the states in the Union, but in no case does that in any way influence the religious facts of the meaning, significance and purposes of the day for Christians.

The Sabbath is and for all time has been the seventh day of the week. The Lord's Day is the first day of the week and has been the Christian's day of worship and service since the establishment of the church.

VII. SUMMARY OF NEW TESTAMENT TEACHING ON WORSHIP

Summarizing the worship of the New Testament church we find that it includes:

1. Preaching and teaching "the apostles' doctrine."

2. Continuing steadfastly in the fellowship of love, service, co-operation and mutual encouragement.

3. Loyalty in assembling around the Lord's Table to commemorate His death and suffering and to recall His resurrection.

4. Continuing "instant in prayer."

5. Sincere and heartfelt adoration and worship of God and Christ in song, prayer and study of the Word.

6. Laying by in store for the Lord's work as He has prospered us.

7. Keeping the Lord's Day sacred to the purposes which were set by apostolic example.

QUESTIONS

1. Under whose guidance was the worship in the New Testament church instituted?

2. Name the four basic elements of this worship.

3. Name three additional features of New Testament worship mentioned in the Epistles.

4. What classes of music are mentioned?

5. What are the New Testament facts as to use of instrumental music with the vocal?

6. Name two features of New Testament worship which passed away with the completion of the written Word.

7. Quote a Scripture which shows that we do not today need prophesyings or speaking in tongues.

8. What does John say as to adding to or taking from the divinely given Word?

9. What day of the week was adopted under apostolic guidance as the special day for Christian assemblage and worship?

10. What names are given the day in the New Testament?

11. Name some of the things that transpired on the first day of the week up to and including apostolic days.

12. Distinguish between the "Sabbath" and the "Lord's Day."

13. Give reasons why the Lord's Day is now the day of Christian worship.

14. Did Constantine change the day? If not, what did he do?

Chapter XII

The Church and Its Fellowship

And they continued stedfastly in the apostles' doctrine and fellowship, and in breaking of bread and in prayers.—Acts 2: 42.

I. IMPORTANCE OF FELLOWSHIP

Remembering that "the fellowship" was one of the four main features of the New Testament worship, it must mean much more than we frequently make of it. The very fact that it is included with the apostles' doctrine, which in turn included all the preaching and teaching and practicing of God's Word, and remembering that this teaching included the whole plan of salvation, would indicate that *fellowship* is of supreme importance. Also, the fact that it is listed with the *communion* and with *prayer* would indicate that it must hold a high place in God's estimate and God's plan. Its very associations mark it for close study.

II. WHAT REALLY IS COMPREHENDED IN THE NEW TESTAMENT TERM?

The word "fellowship" occurs fifteen times in the New Testament. It is used once by Luke (Acts 2: 42), and fourteen times by Paul in the Epistles. It, like the term "faith," is used with more than one implication. The Greek words from which it originated are *koinia*, used fourteen times, and *metache*, used once.

1. The Main Use of the Word.—Most times the term "fellowship" refers to a partnership, a part or place in the worship, a participation in things spiritual, including any work of evangelism, any giving, any praying, any work of mercy, any co-operation in the cause of preaching the gospel, strengthening the brethren or otherwise serving as an active member of the body of Christ. Thus the term practically covers the whole field of Christian life and service.

It eliminates the possibility of a passive faith, an indifferent service or a nonspiritual life. Thus, it stands prominently as a major feature in the Christian scheme.

It is used to refer not only to such a partnership with the brethren, but also to a partnership or participation with God and Christ. A study of New Testament fellowship, therefore, involves a study of Christian attitude toward God and toward the brethren. It involves all Christian work and service. It involves our stewardship of time, talent and means.

I thank my God upon all my remembrance of you, always in every supplication of mine on behalf of you all making my supplication with joy, for your fellowship in furtherance of the gospel from the first day until now.—Phil. 1: 3-5, A.R.V.

If there is therefore any exhortation in Christ, if any consolation of love, if any fellowship of the Spirit, if any tender mercies and compassions, make full my joy, that ye be of the same mind, having the same love, being of one accord, of one mind.—Phil. 2: 1, 2, A.R.V.

That which we have seen and heard declare we unto you also, that ye also may have fellowship with us: yea, and our fellowship is with the Father, and with his Son Jesus Christ.—1 John 1: 3, A.R.V.

2. A Second Use of the Word.—A second use of the word *koinia*, is to refer to the whole body of the church as, "the fellowship." In such cases the definite article is used. The following Scripture would illustrate:

God is faithful, through whom ye were called into the fellowship of his Son Jesus Christ our Lord.—1 Cor. 1: 9, A.R.V.

III. FELLOWSHIP BY MEANS OF OFFERINGS

Now concerning the collection for the saints, as I have given order to the churches of Galatia, even so do ye. Upon the first day of the week let every one of you lay by him in store, as God hath prospered him, that there be no gatherings when I come.—1 Cor. 16: 1, 2.

From Paul's injunction it becomes clear that as the brethren met on the first day of the week they were to "lay by in store as the Lord had prospered them." This referred directly to their contributions. One man a farmer, another a merchant, another a craftsman, having worked at their various trades brought the money thus earned by various people by various skills and cast it into the common treasury for one united purpose. Thus they had fellowship (partnership) in the offering.

Incidentally, this being a prominent part of one of the four features of New Testament worship, it should be done as conscientiously, as reverently and as worshipfully and in the same spirit of devotion as is the reading of the Word, the praying or the participating in the communion. Making the offering is no mercenary break in an otherwise spiritual service of worship. One would thus go to the church assembly not only to hear preaching, pray and commune, but purposely to bring the offering as a part of the divine worship.

IV. The New Testament and Stewardship

Much of Jesus' teaching in sermon and parable was to implant the idea that we are *stewards rather than owners*. Students will easily recall some of these teachings, such as that of "the talents." How is this to be applied to the church of the New Testament today?

1. The Principle Is the Same.—The principle of stewardship as taught by Jesus and the apostles has neither been repealed nor changed. The New Testament is not a book of fast laws as was the law of the Old Testament. The New Testament directions for Christian life consist of principles. To undertake to draw out of the New Testament fixed laws for fixed amounts to be contributed in some fixed way is a hopeless task. Christ is ours and we are Christ's. We and all we have are His. Unless the heart can be imbued with this truth so that we conscientiously administer time, talent and means for Him, because we are Christians, there is little spiritual value in what we call giving.

2. Does the New Testament Teach Political Socialism?— The fact that in the first days of the church in Jerusalem the disciples sold their possessions and had all things in common has led some to presume that the New Testament teaches political socialism as a definite function of Christianity. There is a vast difference.

(a) What this particular group of Christians did was not done by command, law or compulsion.

(b) It was purely voluntary down to the last individual. (Recall the case of Ananias.)

(c) It was not a general political sharing among all people, but a *voluntary* sharing with other *brethren of the church*.

(d) No other such instances are recorded as practiced in any other congregation or locality.

(e) No apostle ever mentions it in his teaching or divinely inspired instructions. It is merely related as a historical instance of a voluntary act on the part of these particular brethren.

(f) One is political and forced from above. The other is spiritual and flows voluntarily from consecrated hearts.

3. Reasons for Giving.—God certainly could have devised ways to carry on His work without our contributions. However, the whole of the gospel plan is devised for our benefit, and is fitted to our human nature. God takes us into partnership. We are to have fellowship with God as well as with our brethren. Jesus announced a principle of human nature when He said, "Where your treasure is, there will your heart be." When men of fifty different vocations each consecrates a part of his ability, time and individual skill to God through the contributions which he makes, there are fifty men who have become in that sense partners with God and fifty men have been drawn closer to God. Giving is naturally not the only way, but is the simplest and easiest way by which fifty men of different walks in life can have fellowship with each other and each with God. When their treasure is truly and reverently consecrated, their hearts and their lives are to that extent consecrated, drawn and bound to Him. Giving is a necessity, not for God, but for us who would grow in grace and knowledge of the truth. It is a form of consecration and service which spreads itself into every working hour of every day of every week. A part of every stroke we make in our work should be consciously for Christ, because we are His.

V. FELLOWSHIP IN SERVICE

While each individual Christian should be an active servant of Christ, and each owes individual service, yet the New Testament pictures "fellowship in service." Much can be achieved by group action. There is an interest and zest to working with others. There is added power. There is added ability for achievement.

VI. FELLOWSHIP IN SUFFERING

Before the New Testament was closed by the writings of John, indescribable suffering had been heaped upon the Christians. Every means of fiendish torture was employed. Unquestionably, the fact that others suffered bravely with staunch and unwavering faith gave courage and strength to each. Paul counted his suffering as a measure of fellowship in the sufferings of Christ.

VII. FELLOWSHIP IN PREACHING

Paul took pride in largely earning his own living, but there is abundant evidence that many Christians from many congregations helped to sustain him and minister to his needs. Thus they had fellowship in his accomplishments. Their names are unknown, but these humble disciples who sustained Paul had a real and vital part in every church he thus planted, just as we who sustain our ministers and missionaries have a real part in every sermon preached and every convert made.

QUESTIONS

1. What indicates the very great importance of ''the fellowship'' as a feature of Christian worship and life?

2. Quote Acts 2: 42.

3. In what two senses is the term ''fellowship'' used in the New Testament? How many times does it occur?

4. As used under its first meaning, ''partnership,'' what features of life and service does it include?

5. Show how our fellowship is with Christ and God as well as with the brethren.

6. Illustrate how Christians have fellowship in their offerings.

7. What spirit or attitude should we have in making our offerings?

8. Quote Paul as to the offerings.

9. What can you say as to the teaching of Jesus and the apostles on stewardship?

10. Distinguish between New Testament principle and Old Testament law on the matter of stewardship.

11. What attitude must accompany a contribution if it is to be a real feature of Christian worship and life?

12. Does the record of sharing as practiced in the Jerusalem church teach political socialism? Distinguish between the two.

13. What are the spiritual and psychological reasons for giving?

14. How can we have fellowship in service? Illustrate.

15. How can we have fellowship in suffering?

16. How can we have fellowship in preaching?

Chapter XIII

The Communion or Lord's Supper

I. NAMES FOR THE COMMUNION

There are six names used to designate the feature of Christian worship, commonly known as the communion. They are:

1. "The Breaking of Bread" (Acts 2:42, 46; 20:7; 1 Cor. 10:16).
2. "The Lord's Supper" (1 Cor. 11:20).
3. "The Communion" (1 Cor. 10:16).
4. "The Lord's Table" (1 Cor. 10:21).
5. "The Sacrament." This term is not found in the New Testament. This is a term applied by the Roman Catholic Church because the communion was supposed to be an oath or vow to the Lord. The Latin word *sacramentum* signified an oath taken by a Roman soldier.
6. "The Eucharist." Neither is this term found in the New Testament. It is a Greek term, and was applied by the Greek Catholic Church. The Greek word *eucharista* meant the giving of thanks. The first four terms are those used by the church of the New Testament.

II. AUTHORITY FOR THE COMMUNION

1. Direct Authority of Christ.—The communion was established by the first Christians under the guidance of the inspired apostles and by the direct authority and command of Christ.

For I say unto you, I shall not drink from henceforth of the fruit of the vine, until the kingdom of God shall come. And he took bread, and when he had given thanks, he brake it, and gave to them, saying, This is my body which is given for you: this do in remembrance of me.

And the cup in like manner after supper, saying, This cup is the new covenant in my blood, even that which is poured out for you.—Luke 22: 18-20, A.R.V.

For I received of the Lord that which also I delivered unto you, that the Lord Jesus in the night in which he was betrayed took bread; and when he had given thanks, he brake it, and said, This is my body, which is for you: this do in remembrance of me. In like manner also the cup, after supper, saying, This cup is the new covenant in my blood: this do, as often as ye drink it, in remembrance of me.—1 Cor. 11: 23-25, A.R.V.

See also Matt. 26: 26-29; Mark 14: 22-25.

Note that both Luke and Paul quote directly from Jesus. Not only is His act related, but the words, *"this do in remembrance of me,"* and *"this do"* could not be more pointedly plain. Here then is the direct authority from Christ Himself, the One in whom rests "all authority."

2. Authority of Apostolic Example.—There are two kinds of authority—primary and delegated. One who has authority can delegate authority to another. Christ chose the apostles, and sent the Holy Spirit of God to guide them in the establishment of His church. Note that under the guidance of all the apostles, the communion was one of the four features of worship as soon as the church was established.

And they continued stedfastly in the apostles' doctrine and fellowship, and in breaking of bread, and in prayers.—Acts 2: 42.

And upon the first day of the week, when the disciples came together to break bread, Paul preached unto them, ready to depart on the morrow; and continued his speech until midnight.—Acts 20: 7.

III. IMPORT OF THE COMMUNION

The emblems (bread and fruit of the vine) stand for the body of Christ sacrificed for us and for His blood shed as the means to redeem us from sin. Thus His broken body and His shed blood are memorialized in the communion just as His burial and resurrection are pictured and memorialized in Christian baptism. Thus the four outstanding and climaxing, as well as the most tragic, events of His earthly career are "shown to the world" in these two Christian ordinances. From the New Testament we learn that:

1. The communion is a definite ordinance of Christ (1 Cor. 11:24).
2. Its observance is, therefore, a test of continued faith and loyalty.
3. It is one of the four prominent phases of Christian worship (Acts 2:42).
4. It is called *His table*, to which He invites all of His own. It is His appointed place for us to meet Him on the Lord's Day (1 Cor. 10:21).
5. It is a monument (memorial) to Christ (1 Cor. 11:26).
6. It is the center of Lord's Day worship (Acts 20:6).
7. It is the pictured story of His sacrifice (1 Cor. 11:26).
8. It is the gospel in epitome.
9. It is the center around which Christians may assemble (Heb. 10:25).
10. It affords the opportunity for Christians to take stock of their progress, forward or backward, at the beginning of each week and to recall that they were buried to the old life and raised to walk the new life. It is, therefore, a place for Christians to ask for forgiveness and to renew their vows to endeavor to live the life in Christ (1 Cor. 11:28).

But let a man examine himself, and so let him eat of that bread, and drink of that cup.—1 Cor. 11:28.

IV. MANNER OF PARTICIPATION

The New Testament makes plain that the *manner* of participation is of profound importance. There is a serious offense committed if we partake "in an unworthy manner."

Wherefore whosoever shall eat the bread or drink the cup of the Lord in an unworthy manner, shall be guilty of the body and the blood of the Lord. But let a man prove himself, and so let him eat of the bread, and drink of the cup. For he that eateth and drinketh, eateth and drinketh judgment unto himself, if he discern not the body. For this cause many among you are weak and sickly, and not a few sleep.—1 Cor. 11:27-30, A.R.V.

Here is a point over which not a few have stumbled. They have "proved" themselves, i. e., examined themselves, to judge whether *they are worthy to partake.* The fact is, *none* is worthy. The word in the Scripture is not "worthy," but "worthily" (or A.R.V., in an unworthy manner). The Scriptures (vv. 29, 30) make plain what the apostle has in mind, in speaking of partaking in "an unworthy manner," "not discerning the body," making of the communion a mere thoughtless ceremony with wits wandering everywhere rather than centering on the sacred emblems and what they signify. The result is given in verse 30, "Many are weak and sickly and not a few sleep."

V. TIME OF OBSERVANCE

The New Testament definitely establishes a time for the observance of the Lord's Supper. However, it should be stated that neither Jesus nor the apostles left any positive command as to the time or frequency. Jesus did not say, "This do ye on each first day of the week." Neither did He say to do it on *any first day* of the week. The matter is established in an entirely different way.

1. Apostolic Example or Precedent.—Jesus did definitely say, "This do." He left many things to be yet accomplished by men whom He chose and who were to be guided by the Holy Spirit whom He promised to send. Among these things were:

(a) The proclaiming of the gospel terms of pardon.

(b) The establishment of the church (Acts 2).

(c) The writing of the New Testament.

(d) The setting of the time for the communion.

From the Scriptures already cited, we may note that they did these things (Acts 20:7).

2. Logical Reasons for the First-day Observance.—

(a) The communion celebrates not only Christ's death and burial, but particularly His resurrection, which took place on the first day of the week.

(b) The Holy Spirit descended and the church was born on the first day of the week.

(c) The fact that the Scriptures call it "the Lord's Day" suggests it as the time for "the Lord's Supper."

(d) Scriptural and apostolic precedent show that the other three of the four features of worship in which they continued steadfastly, i. e., apostles' doctrine, fellowship and prayers, centered on the first day of the week.

3. Each First Day.—Granting that the first day of the week is indicated plainly by the Scriptures, it becomes apparent that each first day as it comes is indicated. Acts 20:7 does not say, "on *a* first day of the week," but "on *the* first day of the week." This was no unusual or spasmodic event. The definite article when so used in all languages always indicates a regularly occurring event. When we say that we celebrate our nation's birthday on *the* fourth of July, it clearly indicates each fourth of July. There certainly is no Scriptural suggestion of a less frequent observance of the Lord's Supper. Practically all Christian bodies have three of the four designated features of New Testament worship each time they meet on the Lord's Day. That is, they have the Scripture teaching and preaching, the offering or fellowship and prayers. There is no more Scriptural ground for any one of these than for any other one. There is no logical reason for having three of these features regularly and one of them occasionally.

VI. WHO SHOULD PARTICIPATE?

Many Scriptures might be cited to determine who should participate in the communion. Two Scriptures already cited are quite sufficient to determine the matter.

1. Acts 2: 37-42 Makes the Matter Plain.—The question to be determined is the antecedent of the pronoun "they" in verse 42. Who are these who continued steadfastly in the breaking of bread. Peter preached Christ. *They* cried out, "What shall *we* do?" Peter replied, "Repent, and be baptized." *"They that gladly received his word* were baptized." "And there were added unto *them about three thousand souls,* and *they* continued stedfastly . . . in the breaking of bread." Very definitely this pronoun refers to those who received the Word, were baptized and were added to the church.

2. Acts 20: 7 Makes the Matter Plain Very Briefly.—"When the *disciples* were gathered together on the first day of the week to break bread."

QUESTIONS

1. What are the various names applied to the communion? Which ones are Scriptural?

2. What are two sources of authority for the communion?

3. Cite Scriptures for each.

4. Enumerate ten things signified by the communion or comprehended in the communion.

5. What Scriptural warning is there as to the manner of participation?

6. How might the manner be wrong?

7. How may one determine the time and frequency of the communion?

8. Who is to participate in the communion? Quote Scriptures.

Chapter XIV

The Church and Prayer

I. Foundation for Prayer in the Church

Jesus, both by word and example, left abundant teaching about prayer as it was to obtain in His church or His kingdom when it should be founded. We must, therefore, give heed to these examples and teachings in the Gospels if we would understand the place, importance and nature of prayer as a feature of the life and worship in the church.

There are very definite features or elements of prayer as taught by Jesus. Among these would be:

1. Absolute sincerity and humility (incident of the publican and Pharisee).
2. Not wordy, but brief and from the heart.

   > But when ye pray, use not vain repetitions, as the heathen do: for they think that they shall be heard for their much speaking.— Matt. 6: 7.

3. Worshipful and never dictatorial.

   > Your Father knoweth what things ye have need of, before ye ask him.—Matt. 6: 8.

4. A prayer for things spiritual.
5. In the spirit of not *my will, but thine.*

   > O my Father, if it be possible, let this cup pass from me: nevertheless not as I will, but as thou wilt.—Matt. 26: 39.

6. In confidence in God as the Father.
7. Never for the purpose of being seen by men. (See Matt. 6: 5.)
8. An ever prayerful attitude. (See Luke 18: 1.)

II. Prayer Definitely Mentioned as One of the Four Chief Features of Worship

Again referring to Acts 2 : 42, where the four chief features of New Testament worship are named, we find prayer, or "the prayers," given as the fourth. These prayers were quite apparently the prayers of *all*. "They" is yet the subject of the sentence and, as we have said before, this pronoun referred to all those who heard the Word, received the Word, obeyed the Word and were added to the church. Jesus had shown by word and example that prayer is a matter so simple that the humblest disciple could pray a prayer quite as acceptable to God as that of the most learned and eloquent. Prayer is a matter for each individual Christian. "They" continued steadfastly in the prayers.

III. New Testament Emphasis on Prayer

Some of the emphasis which Jesus and the apostles put on prayer may be noted from the fact that the word "pray" occurs in the New Testament one hundred and twelve times, and the word "prayer" fifty-three times. A very few times, it is used merely as a word of courtesy from one person to another, such as "I pray thee have me excused." But almost exclusively it is used in the usual sense of talking to God.

IV. For What and for Whom Are We to Pray?

1. Christians are to pray for forgiveness of sins. If we pray sincerely and repentantly we are assured that God *will* forgive again and again.

2. For our enemies and those who despitefully use us (Matt. 5 : 44).

3. For ourselves that we be not tempted (Matt. 26 : 41).

4. For the brethren (Col. 1 : 3 ; Philemon 4).

5. For the sick and afflicted in connection with such helpful remedies as we may be able to administer (Jas. 6 : 13-15).

6. For our ministers and teachers that they may be blessed in the ministry of the Word (2 Thess. 3:1; 1 Thess. 5:25).

7. For personal guidance and strength.

Ask, and it shall be given you; seek, and ye shall find; knock, and it shall be opened unto you: for every one that asketh receiveth; and he that seeketh findeth; and to him that knocketh, it shall be opened.—Matt. 7:7, 8.

V. To Whom Should We Pray?

Prayer is to be made to God in the name of Christ. Prayer to or in the name of human saints is purely a human invention, and is nowhere remotely hinted at in the New Testament.

And in that day ye shall ask me nothing. Verily, verily, I say unto you, Whatsoever ye shall ask the Father in my name, he will give it you.—John 16:23.

Ye have not chosen me, but I have chosen you, and ordained you, that ye should go and bring forth fruit, and that your fruit should remain: that whatsoever ye shall ask of the Father in my name, he may give it you.—John 15:16.

And whatsoever ye shall ask in my name, that will I do, that the Father may be glorified in the Son. If ye shall ask anything in my name, I will do it.—John 14:13, 14.

Only Christ and the Holy Spirit make intercession for us. There is no Scriptural suggestion that deceased saints, including Mary, may do so.

He (the Holy Spirit) maketh intercession for the saints according to the will of God.—Rom. 8:27, A.R.V.

It is Christ . . . who also maketh intercession for us.—Rom. 8:34.

Wherefore he is able also to save them to the uttermost that come unto God by him, seeing he ever liveth to make intercession for them.—Heb. 7:25.

VI. Some of the Ways in Which Prayer Helps

1. Prayer is a form of communion with God. No one can commune with God regularly and not be purified, uplifted and strengthened.

2. It is a source of spiritual growth and development.

3. It is a source of strength in time of temptation.

4. It often brings guidance in times of perplexity.

5. Sincere Christian prayer always brings an answer, sooner or later, and many times the answer is far superior to that for which we have definitely asked.

6. Sincere prayer attunes our souls to God that we may the better hear and understand His Word.

7. Prayer is both subjective and objective. It has an influence on us who pray, but it does not stop at that. Continued, sincere prayers of a Christian never fail to bring a blessing from God. It may come in a form different from what we have pictured and in a way unanticipated, but God does hear and answer the prayers of His own. Both Scripture and Christian experience prove this abundantly.

VI. PRAYER AND FASTING

In a number of cases prayer and fasting are joined in the Scripture text. There is, however, no command or injunction to fast as there is to "repent," "be baptized," "preach the gospel," etc. There is, however, apostolic precedent for fasting under certain conditions. There is no indication of intention that fasting should be obligatory at set times or periods. It appears to be a matter left to the initiative of the individual. In fasting, the body is put under, that the heart may be wholly concentrated on the spiritual.

As they ministered to the Lord, and fasted, the Holy Ghost said, Separate me Barnabas and Saul for the work whereunto I have called them. And when they had fasted and prayed, and laid their hands on them, they sent them away. So they, being sent forth by the Holy Ghost, departed unto Seleucia; and from thence they sailed to Cyprus.—Acts 13: 2-4.

And when they had ordained them elders in every church and had prayed with fasting, they commended them to the Lord, on whom they believed.—Acts 14: 23.

QUESTIONS

1. What preparations are found in the Gospels for instruction as to prayer as a feature in the church?

2. Comment on Jesus and prayer.

3. Name eight essential elements of real prayer.

4. What distinction would you make between ''praying'' and ''saying a prayer''?

5. Name the four basic features of New Testament worship, and show how prayer fits into this gospel plan.

6. Can any Christian pray a real prayer?

7. About how many times do we find the words ''pray'' and ''prayer'' in the New Testament?

8. Name a number of things for which we should pray.

9. For whom should we pray?

10. To whom and in whose name should we pray?

11. Name a large number of ways in which prayer helps.

12. Does the New Testament make fasting obligatory in connection with prayer?

13. Under what circumstances may fasting be spiritually helpful?

Chapter XV

Divine Names for the Church

I. NEW TESTAMENT TEACHING AS TO THE NAME

When we come to study the subject of "the name," we are involved in a double treatment, i. e., the name or names of the church itself and the name or names of the members of the church, i. e., the followers of Christ.

It should also be kept in mind that there is recorded much in the teachings of Christ, as given us in the Gospels, which bears directly on the subject. When we study the names apropos to and in the church, we must be familiar, not only with the history of the church as recorded in Acts and the Epistles, but with the Gospels as well.

II. IS THE MATTER OF THE NAME OF IMPORTANCE?

A somewhat generally expressed, but superficial, thought is that "the name is of minor importance." Our purpose in this study should be to study the New Testament presentation of the matter, and from that determine whether the name is of importance and, if so, what the divinely provided name or names may be. Following are some of the Scriptures on the subject:

1. His name is to be above every name (Phil. 2:9).
2. Salvation is in His name (Acts 4:12; 22:16).
3. We are baptized in His name (Acts 2:38).
4. We are to ask for blessings in His name (John 14:13).
5. All our activities are to be in His name (Col. 3:17).
6. We are blessed when we meet in His name (Matt. 18:20).
7. Unity is in His name (1 Cor. 1:10-13).

8. His name is to be in our foreheads (Rev. 22:4, 5).

9. He prayed that we be kept in His name (John 17).

10. The disciples were called Christians first at Antioch (Acts 11:26).

11. The terms "churches of Christ," "church of God" and "church of the living God" are those used in the New Testament.

This is but a partial list of the Scriptures bearing on the subject, but these are sufficient to indicate that the inspired Scriptures make much of the name and that it behooves us to study the Scriptures most humbly and reverently before assuming that the name which we apply to His church or to His followers is a matter of indifference.

III. Teachings of Christ as to the Name

1. Christ the Sole Owner of the Church.—Christ definitely referred to the church as "my church," which, translated into plain English, means, "church of Christ" or "Christian church." Such is the name that would fittingly be applied.

And I say also unto thee, That thou art Peter, and upon this rock I will build my church; and the gates of hell shall not prevail against it.—Matt. 16:18.

See also Eph. 5:25; Rom. 16:16.

The church is Christ's. He is its Head, its Founder, its sole Owner. The New Testament name clearly brings this fact out and constantly calls attention to it.

2. The Church and the Kingdom.—The terms, "kingdom," "kingdom of heaven," "kingdom of God," etc., appear one hundred and seventeen times in the Gospels and almost exclusively as quoted from the lips of Christ. Remembering that the kingdom on earth and the church are used synonymously in the New Testament, we come to see that "kingdom of God" becomes synonymous with "church of God," and "my kingdom" becomes synonymous with "my church."

IV. THE WRITERS OF ACTS, THE EPISTLES AND REVELATION

1. Titles Found in the English Translations.—When we come to the New Testament record wherein we find the kingdom or church to be definitely established, we find the name appearing as recorded by inspired writers. Some of these instances are:

(a) "The church of God" (Acts 20:28; 1 Cor. 1:2; 11:22; 15:9; 2 Cor. 1:1; 1 Thess. 2:14; 3:5).
(b) "The church of the living God" (1 Tim. 3:15).
(c) "Churches of Christ" (Rom. 16:16).

The term, "the church" or "the churches," occurs ninety-three times exclusive of the above-cited instances. Once, it occurs as "the church of the saints" (1 Cor. 14:33); and once as "the churches of the Gentiles," to distinguish between them and the Jewish churches, but not as a name for the church (Rom. 16:4). Once, it appears as "the churches of Galatia," merely designating a given group of churches, but not as a name.

2. Names of the Church When Translated Into English Expression.—Some have shown a preference between legitimate Scriptural names in English, even to the point of much argument, contention and heat. Largely, this is over the commonly used terms "church of Christ" or "Christian church." There is no occasion for even a difference of opinion if one understands our common usage of the English language.

There was one way in the Greek language to denote ownership or possessorship. That was by using the genitive case ending of the noun. In English there are three ways to express precisely the same idea of ownership or authorship. We may say, "The philosophy of Plato or "The Platonian philosophy." In either case we have expressed exactly the same idea. We might use the third way of expressing ownership and say, "Plato's philosophy." In one case we use the preposition "of"; in another we use "ian," and in the third we use the apostrophe and "s." In all cases we have expressed the same idea. One may use his preference as to how to express it. Likewise, we may say "church of Christ," "Christian church" or "Christ's church." The only difference is as to the form by which we express in English precisely the same idea, i. e., that Christ owns the church, that the church belongs wholly to Him. To indicate that the church belongs to the member or members when we use the term "Christian church," we should have to write it "the Christians' church" or the "church of the Christians."

V. LOGICAL REASONS FOR THE NEW TESTAMENT NAME

1. The church is His "body," and therefore should wear His name (Col. 1:24; Eph. 4:12).

2. The church is His "bride" and should wear the Bridegroom's name (Rev. 21:9; 22:17).

3. The church is a New Testament institution, and as such should wear a New Testament name.

4. The church was named by divine sanction long before any of the many confusing and divisive names were added or substituted, and no one was ever commissioned or authorized to change the name of His church.

VI. NAMES OF THE FOLLOWERS OF CHRIST

1. Old Testament Preparations for the Name.—God named "Israel." This was a definite naming by Jehovah and meant "Prince of God." Otherwise the chosen people would have been mere "Jacobites." In Isa. 62:2, we read the promise of a new name which God was to designate:

And thou shalt be called by a new name, which the mouth of Jehovah shall name.

In Isa. 65:15, A.R.V., we read:

And the Lord Jehovah will slay thee; and he will call his servants by another name.

2. New Testament Fulfillments.—In Acts 11:26 we find: "The disciples were called Christians first in Antioch." Here the promised new name first appears. The Greek word used here for "call" is not the word *kaleo*, which means an ordinary calling, but is *chrematizo*, which means divinely called or called by the will of God. Note that this is a name which is bestowed by the Lord and hence is a divine name.

The name next occurs in Acts 26:28: "And Agrippa said unto Paul, With but little persuasion thou wouldest fain make me a Christian."

Again, the name is used by divine sanction in 1 Pet. 4:16, because here used by the apostle Peter, one divinely inspired. The words are as follows: "But if a man suffer as a Christian, let him not be ashamed; but let him glorify God in this name."

Again, in John 17:11, Jesus Himself pleads in His prayer to the Father that the name may be kept: "Holy Father, keep them in thy name which thou hast given me, that they may be one, even as we are" (A.R.V.).

Again, "Do not they blaspheme the honorable name by which ye are called?" (Jas. 2:7, A.R.V.). "And thou holdest fast my name, and didst not deny my faith. . . ." (Rev. 2:12, A.R.V.).

3. Logical Reasons for the Name "Christian."—

(a) We are to hear the gospel of *Christ*.

(b) We are to believe *in Christ*.

(c) We are to repent *toward Christ*.

(d) We are baptized *into Christ*.

(e) Whatever we do in word or deed is to be done in the *name of Christ*.

(f) His name is to be in our foreheads on the Judgment Day.

(g) When all Christians wear only the common name, "Christian," there is presented a solid front of *unity* rather than *confusion and disunity*.

(h) The name "Christian" honors the Christ rather than sect, creed or party.

(i) This name fulfills the Scriptural teaching that His name is to be "above every name."

(j) The name "Christian," therefore, is not only a divinely given and sanctioned name, but is the logical name for Christ's followers.

4. Other New Testament Names.—The main Scriptural designations of Christ's followers are: "Disciples," "brethren," "saints," "Christians." "Disciples" refers to their relation as learners and followers of Christ. "Brethren" refers to the new relation to each other. "Saints" refers to the new personal condition. "Christians" includes, comprehends and covers all these and more.

The name "disciples" was *not* a *new* name. It had long been used by the Jews, by John the Baptist and by teachers and philosophers. The term "brethren" was not a new name. It had long been used by the Jews, and occurs innumerable times in the Old Testament. The name "saints" was not a new name, but had long been used.

When the disciples were called "Christians" (*chrematizo*, divinely called or named) at Antioch (Acts 11:26), there appeared this name or term for the first time in world history. It was, indeed, a *new* name, fulfilling God's promise.

VII. A SUMMARY

Summarizing the Scriptures, it would appear to be plain that a divinely sanctioned name for the church would be "the church of God," "the church of Christ" or "Christian church" or just, "the church."

When more is added or other names are substituted, division and disunity are indicated, whereas Christ taught and prayed for unity (John 17). The New Testament name calls attention to God and to Christ. If some other name is added or substituted, the names of God and of Christ are obscured and the names and divisions of men emphasized. If we use divinely given New Testament names for the church and for the followers of Christ, we have been loyal to the divine plan and have avoided tampering with things divinely appointed. Divine things should wear the divinely given names.

QUESTIONS

1. In studying "the name," in what double capacity must we consider it?

2. Though the history of the church is found in Acts and the Epistles, why must we also make a study of the Gospels on the subject of the *name?*

3. Does the matter of the *name* really make much difference?

4. Give a number of implications as to the name which may be gathered from the Scriptures.

5. What teachings of Christ throw light on the name which His church should bear?

6. What actual names do we find applied to the church by inspired writers?

7. About how many times does the term "the church" appear in the New Testament?

8. Discuss the relationship of the terms "church of Christ," "Christian church" and "Christ's church."

9. Give a number of logical reasons why Christ's church should bear His name.

10. What are the four most prominent New Testament names for Christ's followers?

11. Which of these was a *new name?*

12. Give logical as well as Scriptural reasons for Christ's followers wearing only the name "Christian."

13. Summarize the Scriptural teachings and implications as to the name for Christ's church and His followers.

Chapter XVI

The Church and Preaching

I. PREACHING AS AN ORDINANCE

Ordinarily we speak of *baptism* and the *communion* as the two New Testament ordinances, in contrast to the seven Roman Catholic ordinances or "sacraments." The "seven sacraments" of the Roman Church are baptism, confirmation, eucharist, penance, extreme unction, orders and matrimony. While the Scriptures may be searched in vain to find where either Christ or the apostles ordered, or ordained, all these ceremonies as ordinances, yet it is certainly true that Christ did ordain, order and command baptism and the Lord's Supper.

Go ye therefore, and teach all nations, baptizing them.—Matt. 28: 19.
This do in remembrance of me.—Luke 22: 19.

The dictionary defines an ordinance as, "That which is decreed or ordained, as by God." The word "ordain" is defined as, "To establish by appointment, decree or law; to enact; especially of the Deity." In this sense there are other ordinances besides the two—baptism and the Lord's Supper. Jesus said, "All authority hath been given unto me in heaven and on earth. Go ye therefore and make disciples of all the nations" (A.R.V.). To *go* and to *teach* are thus definitely ordained by the highest authority. Thus it is that we here treat preaching the gospel as a definite New Testament ordinance. It is a command of Christ to the church. A chief purpose of the church, if not *the* chief purpose, is to see that the gospel is preached to all men everywhere. "Preach the word; be instant in season, out of season; reprove rebuke, exhort."

92

II. Who Is to Do the Preaching?

1. Every Christian Is Responsible.—It is clear that the whole church and every member of it are responsible for seeing that the gospel is preached. It is to be remembered that there is little distinction between *teaching* the gospel and *preaching* the gospel. While not every one can proclaim the gospel effectively in public address, yet any Christian who will can learn to teach it to others. This seems to be the New Testament ideal. The "Go ye" was to all of them. The early disciples so understood it. "Therefore they that were scattered abroad [by the persecutions] went every where preaching the word" (Acts 8:4).

2. Elders, Deacons and Teachers.—An elder, presbyter, bishop or pastor, all of which titles refer to the same office and all of which mean "a shepherd and overseer of the flock," is to be "apt to teach." Stephen and Philip were deacons, and both were most eloquent and successful preachers of the Word. Priscilla taught Apollos the way of the Lord more perfectly. These and many other examples which might be drawn from the Scriptures show that preaching the gospel is not to be confined to but a few public proclaimers of the Word, and certainly not to a special clerical class.

3. Full-time Specialists in Public Proclamation.—The New Testament makes it abundantly plain that many shall devote their whole life and energy to the proclamation of the gospel, and that these should go far and near and be sustained by the church.

How then shall they call on him in whom they have not believed? And how shall they believe in him of whom they have not heard? And how shall they hear without a preacher? And how shall they preach, except they be sent?—Rom. 10: 14, 15.

They which preach the gospel should live of the gospel.—1 Cor. 9: 14.

Assuredly gathering that the Lord had called us for to preach the gospel unto them.—Acts 16: 10.

Whereunto I am ordained a preacher, and an apostle . . . a teacher of the Gentiles in faith and verity.—1 Tim. 2: 7.

It pleased God by the foolishness of preaching to save them that believe.—1 Cor. 1: 21.

III. The New Testament Church a Preaching Church

The very essence of the New Testament church is that it is a preaching church as contrasted to the religions of ritualistic performances, either heathen or Christian. Ceremony and ritual had exhausted themselves in Judaism and in the heathen religions. The church house today should be built for preaching and teaching rather than for the mere repetition of rituals. By rituals we do not refer to the divinely appointed ordinances. "The gospel is the power of God unto salvation." Mere priest-craft has little place in New Testament Christianity. Images, saints, relics, holy waters, holy candles, novenas, etc., which make of the house of God a place of concealed mysteries rather than à place for the revealing of the gospel—all this is a far departure from the picture given of the church in the New Testament.

IV. What Is to Be Preached?

Preach the word; be urgent in season, out of season; reprove, rebuke, exhort, with all longsuffering and teaching.—2 Tim. 4: 2, A.R.V.

But though we, or an angel from heaven, preach any other gospel unto you than that which we have preached unto you, let him be accursed.—Gal. 1: 8.

But we preach Christ crucified, unto the Jews a stumblingblock, and unto the Gentiles foolishness; but unto them that are called, both Jews and Greeks, Christ the power of God, and the wisdom of God.—1 Cor. 1: 23, 24, A.R.V.

And began at the same scripture, and preached unto him Jesus.—Acts 8: 35.

For I determined not to know any thing among you, save Jesus Christ, and him crucified.—1 Cor. 2: 2.

The point to these Scriptures is that the New Testament church is to preach *the* gospel, not merely *a* gospel or not merely to preach. Preaching might, and too often does, consist of mere lectures on various themes—social, political or literary—and may be wholly devoid of any gospel at all.

Again we might preach *a* gospel. There are many such devised of men, some of which are often patterned, at least in part, after the teachings of the Bible. A gospel usually is the exploitation of one idea, often seeking a following for one man or restricted group.

The gospel seeks only the glory of Christ, proclaims the whole truth of Christ as divinely revealed, seeks to win men to Christ rather than to party or sect and is preached as a message divine. Preaching the gospel involves the proclamation or delivery of a message which has already been given rather than a message left to be devised by human authors.

V. WHERE, WHEN AND TO WHOM IS THE GOSPEL TO BE PREACHED?

1. Where Shall the Gospel Be Preached?—Naturally, the answer to the question as to where the gospel is to be preached is, Throughout the whole world. This answer is too general to cover specific instances. Certainly the Scriptures call for preaching the gospel to all people in all lands, including our own. But should the gospel preaching be strictly confined to consecrated pulpits in stated buildings and to fixed places and set times? Paul and Silas preached in the jail and by the riverside. Paul preached from the Areopagus in Athens, in the Jewish synagogues in numberless cities and in his prison house in Rome. Peter preached in the house of Cornelius. Ananias preached to Paul in Paul's private room in Damascus. There is danger today, since we have builded so many church houses of brick and stone, that we say "come" and stop at that. We must remember that Christ says "go." There is danger that we may fence the gospel in and fence the unsaved out. Too much dressing may hide and obscure the gospel.

2. When Shall It Be Preached?—Jesus preached to the Samaritan woman at *lunch time,* when He was *on a journey,* when He was *weary and thirsty.* Paul preached to Felix when *in court* on trial for his life. The apostles preached *in the temple* and *in the synagogues.* Preaching under New Testament precedent was not confined to a fixed hour in the week, but took advantage of every opportunity and saw opportunity everywhere.

3. To Whom Shall It Be Preached?—To employ the available force of preachers and usurp their time to preach to and for congregations of people who are already Christians is not in keeping with New Testament ideals. Jesus said,

> For the Son of man is come to seek and to save that which was lost.— Luke 19: 10.
> As my Father hath sent me, even so send I you.—John 20: 21.

Jesus gave as one of His chief credentials that the poor had the gospel preached unto them.

> And said unto him, Art thou he that should come, or do we look for another? Jesus answered and said unto them, Go and shew John again those things which ye do hear and see: The blind receive their sight, and the lame walk, the lepers are cleansed, and the deaf hear, the dead are raised up, and the poor have the gospel preached to them.—Matt. 11: 3-5.

While it is true that preaching should be done to the saints to build them up in Christ, yet we should never lose sight of the fact that the gospel is to be preached to the lost.

VI. MOTIVES FOR PREACHING THE GOSPEL

It is true that Paul commended preaching even when it was done out of envy. However, it was the fact that Christ was preached that he commended and not the motive. There can be but one proper motive. That motive must be one that grows out of a love for God and Christ, a conviction of divine truth that must be proclaimed and a sincere passion to serve.

Mere professionalism in the ministry has been a serious bane to the cause of Christ. Paul said, "Woe is unto me if I preach not the gospel." This reveals one phase of Paul's motive.

For if I preach the gospel, I have nothing to glory of; for necessity is laid upon me; for woe is unto me, if I preach not the gospel. For if I do this of mine own will, I have a reward: but if not of mine own will, I have a stewardship intrusted to me.—1 Cor. 9: 16, 17, A.R.V.

Some one has named a true preacher of the gospel as, "The herald of a passion." Another wise preacher advised a young man as follows: "Do not become a preacher unless you can not help it." By this he meant that one must have such a knowledge and conviction of the truth that he is compelled to proclaim it. This would rule out professional clericalism, whatever its motive—whether the prospect of a soft life, the desire for emulation by men, the desire to stand in front and be heard or whatever the human motive might be. Those who have given their lives to preaching need again and again to examine their motive.

VII. TRAINING FOR PREACHING

The souls of men are at stake and are precious enough that one who would preach the gospel to save men must have a conscience that will drive him to equip himself to preach so that the gospel may win men. Mere desire and even proper motives are not sufficient. Ignorant manhandling of the Scriptures may lose souls rather than save. The motive must be so strong that one's whole strength is devoted to attaining skill in "handling aright the word of truth." The gospel is God's dynamite (*dynamis*, translated "power"). One must learn how to handle it. There is New Testament precedent. Paul trained Timothy most carefully, and instructed Titus and others. Mere training is not enough. University degrees in psychology, philosophy and science are not a guarantee that one is trained in mind and heart in the living Word of God.

QUESTIONS

1. What two features are usually called the ''Christian ordinances''?
2. What sectarian additions have been added?
3. What is an ordinance?
4. Quote a Scripture showing preaching and teaching the gospel to be an ordinance.
5. Who is commanded to preach?
6. Quote a Scripture or Scriptures showing that some should give their whole time to preaching while being sustained by others.
7. What is the first main function of the church?
8. Contrast a preaching church with one which depends on a ritualistic program.
9. What is to be preached?
10. Contrast preaching *the* gospel, preaching *a* gospel and mere *preaching*.
11. Where should preaching be done?
12. When should preaching be done?
13. To whom should preaching be done?
14. What is a proper motive for preaching?
15. Discuss training to preach.

The Church and Evangelism

I. EVANGELISM AND MISSIONS

The New Testament can be searched in vain to find any distinction between "evangelism" and what has more recently been called "missions, home and foreign." The New Testament very definitely provides for evangelizing, i. e., preaching the gospel to all unevangelized people everywhere, whether near or far. A study of the New Testament would lead us to define "evangelism" as "The use of the Word of God by as nearly as possible every Christian, to win to Christ, as nearly as possible, every one who is not a Christian." Various methods are portrayed, including the mass evangelistic effort as on Pentecost; numerous cases of what might be termed "personal evangelism," as the Philippian jailer, Lydia and others; "home evangelism," such as the case of Cornelius, etc. Paul's long journeys through Asia and Europe were evangelistic journeys.

It is for these reasons that we include what might be treated as "The New Testament Church and Missions" under the title, "The New Testament Church and Evangelism."

II. CHRIST AND EVANGELISM

1. The Great Commission.

Go ye therefore, and make disciples of all the nations, baptizing them into the name of the Father and of the Son and of the Holy Spirit; teaching them to observe all things whatsoever I commanded you: and lo, I am with you always, even unto the end of the world—Matt. 28: 19, 20, A.R.V.

And he said unto them, Go ye into all the world, and preach the gospel to the whole creation. He that believeth and is baptized shall be saved; but he that disbelieveth shall be condemned.—Mark 16: 15, 16, A.R.V.

And that repentance and remission of sins should be preached in his name unto all the nations, beginning from Jerusalem. Ye are witnesses of these things. And behold, I send forth the promise of my Father upon you: but tarry ye in the city, until ye be clothed with power from on high.—Luke 24: 47-49, A.R.V.

Here is the direct word of the Master, and certainly here is a plain commission to evangelize. These records, given us by the three writers, present indications that they are the reports of three separate occasions on which Jesus gave the same command in substance but in different words.

2. Jesus' Earthly Teaching.—Aside from the plain commission above, be it remembered that large numbers of Jesus' teachings were definite suggestions on evangelism. For a few examples, recall the parable of the feast and the folk of the "highways and byways," also the parable of "the sower," the parable of "the draught of fishes, great and small," and numerous other direct illustrations of what was to be done.

III. The Church Was Born in Evangelism

One need but to read in Acts 2 the story of the birthday of the church in Jerusalem, when "three thousand were added to them," to be convinced that evangelism is a definite and fixed feature of Christ's program. If Christ and the inspired apostles did not know who was to be reached and how, then the whole of our faith is in vain.

IV. The Records in Acts and the Epistles

Go with Philip down to hated Samaria or stand with Stephen before a hating mob in Jerusalem, and who will fail to catch not only the message preached, but the passion and spirit with which it was preached. Travel with Paul for twenty years through perils on land and on sea, perils among heathen enemies raised to mob fury as in Ephesus, or perils among those who were his own Jewish brethren wherein he was driven out of city after city. Stand with Paul on the steps of the Tower of Antonio, in Jerusalem, faced by a mob sworn neither to eat nor drink until they had killed him. Read again the wondrous messages of Paul's Epistles, and remember that they were written by hands manacled for the one crime of persistently evangelizing the unevangelized. Travel with Barnabas, Mark, Luke, Timothy and Titus as they gave their lives to one work and one cause, which was the carrying of the gospel message to those who knew Him not. Walk with James and Peter and Paul on their last short walk on earth to a martyr's death. Such a New Testament journey can not possibly fail to convince any one that the New Testament church was and is an evangelistic church primarily and definitely.

When a church loses the evangelistic urge, purpose and spirit it loses the very spirit of the church of the New Testament, and becomes but an insipid copy of human social organizations. What a travesty on Christ when a church bearing His name becomes a place for a mere weekly dress parade, a place to have the conscience salved by meaningless performance and the ears tickled by the sound of sonorous platitudes!

V. NOT ONLY THE APOSTLES, BUT THE DEACONS AND ALL THE DISCIPLES EVANGELIZED

As we study the New Testament we find that the work of the church was not delegated to a relatively small clerical class. Stephen, the first Christian martyr for evangelism, was a deacon. Philip, who went first to the hated Samaritans and turned hosts of them to Christ and who later taught the Ethiopian and thus started the gospel on its way into Africa, was a deacon.

The disciples, when they were scattered abroad by the reign of death and terror in Jerusalem and Judea, ''went everywhere

preaching the word.'' Men of Cyprus carried the Word to
and planted the great church in Antioch of Syria. Unknown
brethren carried the message to Rome, made converts and established the church there long before Paul ever entered the city.
This again gives a picture of what a New Testament church is
really like.

VI. Preaching and Evangelism

In the chapter preceding this one we studied ''The New
Testament Church and Preaching.'' In this we are studying
''The New Testament Church and Evangelism.'' These subjects
called for a separate study, but now it will appear that they are
so closely bound together that they seem to be almost identical.
Evangelism certainly calls for preaching to one or many, and
New Testament preaching as certainly aims at evangelizing. Evangelistic preaching is gospel preaching tempered to
the specific aim of breaking through the solid walls of indifference, penetrating to the very hearts of sinners, stirring the
conscience and moving recalcitrant human wills. Evangelistic
preaching calls for a solid conviction on the part of the preacher,
for only conviction can produce conviction. It calls for fervor,
i. e., fire, for only fire can warm cold hearts. It calls for
faith in both God and man. Only faith can beget faith, and
without faith in man, preaching would be pointless.

VII. Preachers Are Evangelists

A study of the New Testament reveals that the New Testament church was made up of ''disciples,'' ''brethren,'' ''saints,''
''Christians.'' All these terms refer to the total membership.
Then there were apostles, prophets, elders, deacons, teachers
and evangelists. The apostles and prophets passed away, being
no longer needed when their special work of establishing the
church and giving us the written Word had been completed.

We have, therefore, today, elders, deacons, teachers and evangelists or preachers. There are four names used in the New

Testament for the office which is now usually designated by the one term "elder." These New Testament names are elders, presbyters, bishops and pastors. All refer to the same office or work. These were all local, and the office was one of oversight, spiritual guidance and safeguarding of the local flock. The various terms had a slight shading of difference in meaning. Elder and presbyter referred to the fact that they were to be of the more seasoned in Christian life and experience. Bishop and pastor meant shepherd, overseer or safeguarder of the flock.

The work of the evangelist or preacher is to preach the Word. All too often in our modern-day adjustments the all-too-small supply of evangelists or preachers have become mere subsidized elders, bishops or pastors, to the disadvantage of preaching or evangelizing. In a strictly New Testament church, or one which aspires to be such, the people and preacher should remember that the preacher is an evangelist and not a mere feeder and overseer of the flock.

VIII. EVANGELISM BY THE PRINTED WORD

There is one advantage and legitimate feature of a New Testament church today which was little in evidence in the first days of the church. That feature is the printed Word. To this perhaps should be added the multiplied voice of radio. In Paul's day he sent hand-written communications to the churches and these were painstakingly hand-copied. Today, a New Testament church may avail itself of unlimited and inexpensive copies of the printed Word and of teaching through printed tracts which proclaim the gospel, and, likewise, printed sermons and teachings in books and Christian periodicals. These advantages a New Testament church of today has over the church of the first centuries. In the spirit of the church of the first century, the church should lay hold of and use to the fullest these added facilities for spreading the gospel message to all people.

QUESTIONS

1. What can you say of evangelism and missions as presented in the New Testament?

2. Quote the Great Commission and show that it is strictly an evangelistic commission given by the Lord.

3. What can you say of Christ's earthly teaching on evangelism?

4. Under what atmosphere was the church launched?

5. Give instances from Acts and the Epistles showing the relation of evangelism to a New Testament church.

6. What is the result if a congregation called Christian loses the evangelistic spirit?

7. Give Scriptural examples of deacons and plain disciples evangelizing.

8. What special characteristics does evangelistic preaching have?

9. In the New Testament scheme, what is the preacher's place and work?

10. How may the printed Word be used in evangelism today as it could not be used in the day of Paul?

Chapter XVIII

The Church and the Holy Spirit

I. DIFFICULTIES INVOLVED

1. The Infinite and the Finite.—It should be remembered that the Bible treats of God and of man. It therefore treats of the Infinite and the finite. It treats of time and eternity. In the saving of the soul, both God and man are involved. Therefore, the Bible deals both with what God does and with what man is to do. This latter is naturally plain and wholly understandable as it must be if man is to be responsible. In treating this phase it is relatively easy to present the matter plainly.

2. Impossible to Comprehend the Infinite.—When we come to treating of God or God's part in salvation, however, we are dealing with the Infinite, which we finite mortals may not hope to comprehend. Comprehend means to surround or take in. If we could comprehend God wholly, we should be equal to or even greater than God in wisdom and understanding.

In studying the Holy Spirit we are dealing with one of the manifestations of God. Hence the difficulty and even impossibility of a presentation that is clear and conclusive.

3. A Proper Approach to Scriptural Statements About Manifestations of Deity.—It is for the above reasons, perhaps, that diverse teachings, theories, explanations and theologies have all too often been put forth and confusion has frequently resulted. It therefore behooves us to stick humbly and faithfully to Scriptural terms and Scriptural statements on the subject of the Holy Spirit, and, as Abraham Lincoln put it, "Take all of it we can on reason and the rest on faith," recognizing that we mortals are laboring to comprehend the nature and works of the Infinite.

The Bible tells us that there are the Father, Son and Holy Spirit and that "these three are one." Trinitarians and Unitarians have argued and multiplied words through the centuries to try to reconcile what appears to be unreconcilable, and yet they have added not one word of clarity to the original Scriptural statement. Faith can only look forward to the day when, freed of mortal hamperings, we may easily understand. This is the field of faith. Meantime, we can rest on the Scriptural statement that there is a heavenly Father, God; the Son, Jesus Christ our Saviour, and the Holy Spirit, and that "these three are one."

II. Some Things That Are Plain as to the Holy Spirit

The term, "Holy Spirit," is used sixty-six times in the New Testament aside from numerous uses of the terms, "Spirit" and "Spirit of God." From these many references we learn some things.

1. The Holy Spirit Is a Definite Personality Who Is One With the Father and Who Teaches.

2. The Holy Spirit Is a Guide.—Jesus definitely promised to send the Holy Spirit as a guide to impart to or reveal to the chosen apostles all truth, and to call to their remembrance all that He had taught them. These revealed truths they wrote down, and we have the Holy-Spirit-inspired Word as our guide today. We may be as sure of what to do to be saved as we could be if Peter, John and Paul could tell us directly by word of mouth.

The Holy Spirit is none the less our one Guide today, though He may employ a different method. He guided these inspired men through direct inspiration; He guides us through the inspired Word. Whatever theories any one may have or whatever work the Holy Spirit may do in the conversion of men and in the comforting and guidance of Christians, we are resting on safe and solid ground that is unquestioned as long as we go for guidance and instruction to the written Word of God, which is the Word of the Holy Spirit. Anything or any theory or teaching, however, which is contrary to the Word or which ignores the Word by substituting human opinion or human experience for the clear statement of the Word is clearly not the voice of the Spirit of God. Neither the Father nor the Holy Spirit contradicts one another.

These things have I spoken unto you, while yet abiding with you. But the Comforter, even the Holy Spirit, whom the Father will send in my name, he shall teach you all things, and bring to your remembrance all that I said unto you.—John 14: 25, 26, A.R.V.

We suggest that the entire passage, John 14: 15-26, be read.

Nevertheless I tell you the truth: It is expedient for you that I go away; for if I go not away, the Comforter will not come unto you; but if I go, I will send him unto you. And he, when he is come, will convict the world in respect of sin, and of righteousness, and of judgment: of sin, because they believe not on me; of righteousness, because I go to the Father, and ye behold me no more; of judgment, because the prince of this world hath been judged.—John 16: 7-11, A.R.V.

3. The Holy Spirit Is a Comforter of Christians.

And hope putteth not to shame; because the love of God hath been shed abroad in our hearts through the Holy Spirit which was given unto us.—Rom. 5: 5, A.R.V.

See also John 16: 7-11, above.

4. The Holy Spirit Is One Who May Be Resisted and Grieved.

Ye stiffnecked and uncircumcised in heart and ears, ye do always resist the Holy Spirit: as your fathers did, so do ye.—Acts 7: 51, A.R.V.

And grieve not the Holy Spirit of God, in whom ye were sealed unto the day of redemption.—Eph. 4: 30, A.R.V.

Quench not the Spirit.—1 Thess. 5: 19, A.R.V.

5. The Spirit Makes Intercession for Us Before the Throne of God.—Not only our Saviour Jesus Christ intercedes for His own, but also does the Holy Spirit.

Likewise the Spirit also helpeth our infirmities: for we know not what we should pray for as we ought: but the Spirit itself maketh intercession for us with groanings which cannot be uttered.—Rom. 8: 26.

How these things may be, or how accomplished, we may not understand, but we have God's Word and God's promise. This we *can* understand.

III. THREE MANIFESTATIONS OF THE SPIRIT

Some of the confusion in thinking and teaching as to the Holy Spirit may be removed if we note that the New Testament quite apparently presents at least three distinct manifestations of the Holy Spirit and His work. These are, the *baptism* or enduement of the Holy Spirit, the *special gifts* of the Holy Spirit and the *general gift* of the Holy Spirit. The confusion of teaching on the subject has arisen largely by a failure to note these distinctions. In studying the Scriptures, the questions should be raised, To whom were these promises made by Christ and the Spirit Himself? For what time were they made and for what purpose?

1. The Baptism of the Holy Spirit.—In general, the baptism of the Holy Spirit or enduement with power was to a chosen group to prepare them to proclaim the gospel by word of mouth and later to write it down once and for all. As a mark of this special divine guidance, they were granted, or had bestowed upon them "power from on high," i. e., power to perform miracles, heal the sick and lame, raise the dead, speak in tongues, interpret and prophesy.

This was necessary in the beginning when there was no written Word of the new dispensation. These marks were bestowed so that when Peter or John or Paul or others on whom the gift of prophecy and inspiration was bestowed spoke and, later, wrote, men might know they spoke as the voice of God.

When the Word had been proclaimed and later written, these special enduements of powers resulting from the baptism of the Holy Spirit were no longer needed. The promise or prophecy made by John that "he that cometh after me . . . shall baptize you in the Holy Spirit" was definitely fulfilled in these chosen mouthpieces of the most high God. There is and has been practically no difference of opinion as to that fact.

Some have looked upon this promise of baptism in the Holy Spirit by the Lord as a general promise to all Christians. Be it noted, however, that this manifestion of the Holy Spirit carried with it miraculous powers and special functions. The baptism of the Holy Spirit was one to be administered by the Lord Himself. It was for a specific purpose, to fill a need in a specific time, and was, therefore, bestowed upon those chosen to fulfill a specific work within that time. There are two clear-cut examples of this baptism:

And, being assembled together with them, he charged them not to depart from Jerusalem, but to wait for the promise of the Father, which, said he, ye heard from me: for John indeed baptized with water; but ye shall be baptized in the Holy Spirit not many days hence.—Acts 1: 4, 5, A.R.V.

And they were all filled with the Holy Spirit, and began to speak with other tongues, as the Spirit gave them utterance.—Acts 2: 4, A.R.V.

While Peter yet spake these words, the Holy Spirit fell on all them that heard the word. And they of the circumcision that believed were amazed, as many as came with Peter, because that on the Gentiles also was poured out the gift of the Holy Spirit. For they heard them speak with tongues, and magnify God.—Acts 10: 44-46, A.R.V.

2. The Special Gifts of the Holy Spirit.—Among other powers bestowed upon these chosen ones who were baptized in the Holy Spirit was the power to impart to others special powers by prayer and the laying on of hands. These imparted gifts included the power of prophecy, the ability to speak in tongues and to interpret. These are sometimes called, "The extraordinary gifts of the Spirit." They differed in a number of respects from the baptism of the Holy Spirit. The former was administered by the Lord, while these gifts were imparted by the laying on of the hands of those who had been baptized in the Holy Spirit. Those baptized in the Holy Spirit had the power to impart these extraordinary gifts to others, but these others did not have the power to pass them on to still others.

These gifts were similar to the gifts accompanying the baptism of the Holy Spirit in one respect. They were temporary. That is, they were needed in the day when the churches were being founded and the gospel spread abroad before the written Word was completed. These gifts, like the gifts imparted to the apostles, passed away when the need had passed and when the last apostle and the last one to whom the apostles had imparted these gifts had passed away.

> Now when the apostles that were at Jerusalem heard that Samaria had received the word of God, they sent unto them Peter and John: who, when they were come down, prayed for them, that they might receive the Holy Spirit: for as yet it was fallen upon none of them: only they had been baptized into the name of the Lord Jesus. Then laid they their hands on them, and they received the Holy Spirit.—Acts 8: 14-17, A.R.V.

Here is an example of something these apostles had the power to do which Philip could not do:

> And when Paul had laid his hands upon them, the Holy Spirit came on them; and they spake with tongues, and prophesied.—Acts 19: 6, A.R.V.
>
> Neglect not the gift that is in thee, which was given thee by prophecy, with the laying on of the hands of the presbytery.—1 Tim. 4: 14, A.R.V.

In this case, the gift that was in Timothy was imparted "by prophecy," accompanied by the laying on of "the hands of the presbytery" (elders). It is altogether possible that these presbyters had received the baptism of the Holy Spirit. Note that in the New Testament the word "apostle" is used at times to designate a larger group than the original twelve.

3. The General or Ordinary Gift of the Holy Spirit.

Repent ye, and be baptized *every one of you* in the name of Jesus Christ unto the remission of your sins; and ye shall receive the gift of the Holy Spirit.—Acts 2: 38, A.R.V.

Here plainly is the statement of an inspired apostle that all who believe, repent and obey the gospel are to ''receive the gift of the Holy Spirit.'' This quite apparently is not to those of that day and place only, but ''to all that are afar off,'' Gentiles as well as Jews. That includes all today who hear and obey the gospel.

The only question is, What is implied in this general gift of the Holy Spirit? To conclude that this promised gift is identical with the baptism of the Holy Spirit or with the special gifts bestowed by the apostles would imply that all who become Christians today may expect to be able to speak in tongues, interpret, prophesy, heal the sick, raise the dead and even speak for God by adding to His Word. Quite apparently such is not intended to be promised. What is promised? While we may not now know or understand all the blessings involved in this precious gift, yet the Scriptures make plain that at least the following is promised and to be expected:

(a) The Holy Spirit's clear Word, as recorded in the New Testament, which is ours for all time and all occasions (John 14: 26; 2 Tim. 3: 16).

(b) His indwelling presence within us to comfort, inspire, encourage and guide (John 16: 7-11; 1 Cor. 6: 19).

(c) His sanctifying influence (1 Cor. 6: 11).

(d) His guidance in times of perplexity, through the Word and directly through prayer (2 Tim. 2: 15).

(e) His intercession for us before God's throne (Rom. 8: 26).

(f) His assurance of forgiveness through the definite promise of God (1 Thess. 1: 5).

(g) His revealed promise of eternal life and heaven (1 John 2: 25).

(h) The Spirit dwelling in us bears precious fruit, every item of which is an unmeasurable blessing.

> But the fruit of the Spirit is love, joy, peace, longsuffering, kindness, goodness, faithfulness, meekness, self-control; against such there is no law.—Gal. 5: 22, A.R.V. (Note that among these fruits of the Spirit within us, the last named is "self-control" rather than noisy and unrestrained maunderings.)

(i) The Spirit works through us. Jesus said, "The works that I do . . . ye shall do greater." Jesus fed a few thousand people. Today, the Holy Spirit working in and through Christians feeds millions of the hungry. Because of the Holy Spirit in Christians, the earth is belted with Christian hospitals ministering to and healing millions of the sick, compared with the relatively few healed by Jesus personally. Jesus preached in a territory fifty by seventy miles in extent. Today, the Holy Spirit in Christians preaches in over 900 tongues to men of every race and nation around the world. Jesus raised Lazarus from the dead only to live a few more years and die again. The Holy Spirit, given to Christians and working through them is bringing *eternal life* to uncounted millions. These are but a few examples of the things involved in this wonderful gift of the Holy Spirit promised to all Christians. How we have failed to appraise and appreciate that which was promised and recorded in Acts 2: 38!

Could even God bestow a greater gift upon His children than all that is comprehended in these unmeasured blessings? Temporary speakings in tongues, healings or prophesyings are not equal to this gift which is promised to all. Thus what is often called "the ordinary gift" turns out to be the *extraordinary* gift. The only failure would be our failure to appropriate this priceless gift promised to all, to use it for our spiritual growth and employ it for the service in the church.

IV. The Sin Against the Holy Spirit

Therefore I say unto you, Every sin and blasphemy shall be forgiven unto men; but the blasphemy against the Spirit shall not be forgiven. And whosoever shall speak a word against the Son of man, it shall be forgiven him; but whosoever shall speak against the Holy Spirit, it shall not be forgiven him, neither in this world, nor in that which is to come.— Matt. 12: 31, 32, A.R.V.

Here is the one unforgivable sin—the sin against the Holy Spirit. If we reject or disregard His Word, refuse or neglect His guidance and refuse an abode in our hearts for the Spirit of God, how could we be forgiven? Every means of pardon, forgiveness and salvation has been rejected, and every portal to God's heaven has been shut. Forgiveness has been forever forfeited. This sin is the unforgivable sin.

QUESTIONS

1. What difficulty is involved in studying things pertaining to the Almighty, His works and His manifestations?

2. What fact has led to confusion in teachings as to the Holy Spirit?

3. What is a good rule to follow in the study of this subject?

4. Name some of His works that show that the Holy Spirit is a personality.

5. Through what two ways does the Holy Spirit serve as our guide?

6. How can and does the Holy Spirit guide us as definitely and surely today in the matters of salvation as He did men on Pentecost?

7. In what two ways does the Holy Spirit come to us to bring comfort?

8. How may we resist and grieve the Holy Spirit?

9. Who, aside from Jesus, makes intercession for us?

10. What are the three manifestations of the Spirit?

11. Which of these were for a special purpose at a special time?

12. Why was this necessary at that time?

13. Why not necessary now?

14. What similarity and what differences are there between the baptism of the Holy Spirit and the special gifts of the Holy Spirit?

15. To whom is the general gift of the Holy Spirit promised?

16. Name eight things comprehended in this gift to all.

17. What is the unforgivable sin and why is it unforgivable?

Chapter XIX

The Church of the New Testament and Its Organization

I. SIMPLICITY OF THE NEW TESTAMENT CHURCH ORGANIZATION

First of all may we say that the New Testament does not present any plan or suggestion of organization such as the complex organizations with ranks of prelates which we see today in many churches. Such a plan as the New Testament presents is decidedly simple. The New Testament church, as presented, is rather a living *organism* than a complex organization. The carrying on of its appointed task depended more largely upon the faith, love, loyalty, life and spirit of all its members than upon any kind of complex machinery.

1. What We Mean by Legitimate Organization.—Organization merely means the distribution and assignment of tasks so that the whole work of any group, such as the church or a congregation, may best be carried out. Under the New Testament, therefore, there may be two legitimate phases of organization as follows:

(a) Such organization as is definitely suggested in the New Testament, such as elders, deacons, teachers and evangelists.

(b) Such further division of phases of the work, distribution of tasks and assignments of duties as may assist in carrying out the Great Commission in good order and effectively. The New Testament leaves the way open for Christians to exercise their minds, their loyalty and initiative. It permits them to devise such means as may be effective as long as these means, agencies or plans are not anti-Scriptural or as long as they do not usurp divine prerogatives, substitute human authority for the authority of Christ, imperil individual liberty in Christ or crush out or obscure the spirit and divine purpose of the church by overshadowing machinery and human devices.

2. Tendencies of Man in Organization.—The tendency of human organization is to glorify men and aggrandize the organization itself. The tendency of organizations devised by men is to perpetuate the organization for the sake of the organization and for the sake of the place and power in the hands of officials. This is wholly foreign to the New Testament spirit as well as letter and plan. Such an organization as that which designates any mere man as "Lord God the Pope" (Father) or "Vicegerent of Christ," placing him at the head with supreme authority over the church, the churches and all the people in the church is not only un-Scriptural, but anti-Scriptural. When there is added to this an organization with cardinals, archbishops, bishops and priests, each invested with similar authority, every one of the provisos mentioned above has been violated. Ecclesiastical organizations less complete, but retaining the same general idea of authority over the churches are no different from the Roman Church organization except in degree. The departure from New Testament provisions and principles is still maintained.

II. An Organism Versus an Organization

1. Characteristics of an Organism.—We have said that the New Testament conception is an organism rather than an organization. The characteristic of any organism is that it is something that is vital, growing and functioning in every part. Another characteristic of an organism is that when any part or member ceases to be needed, it is automatically eliminated. The church is compared to a vine. The members are the branches calculated to bear fruit. The church is compared to a human body, the members being the members of the body, such as an eye, a hand, a foot. When a member ceases to function, it is automatically eliminated in an organism. This is not necessarily or often true of an organization. Once built, the tendency is to maintain its every part whether useful or harmful, merely for the purpose of maintaining place, power, prestige or pelf. Hence the complex and cumbersome organizations today, many of which constitute the strongest bulwark for maintaining division.

2. A New Testament Example.—Be it noted that in the New Testament church, when even apostles, prophets and inspired men had served their divinely given task and were no longer needed, they automatically were eliminated, leaving in perpetuity only those means and offices which in perpetuity are and will be needed to carry out the Great Commission; namely, the written Word of God, evangelists (preachers), elders, deacons, teachers and plain Christians.

The problem of organization today is to find how best to direct and use these so that each may function as divinely intended and bear the fruit intended.

III. PECULIARITY OF ORGANIZATION DELINEATED IN THE NEW TESTAMENT

1. New Testament Organization Strictly Local.—One who peruses the New Testament will search in vain for any hint of an organization other than that applying to a local church. The terms elder, bishop, pastor and presbyter were used synonymously. The office of an elder, bishop, pastor or presbyter was the same office and was local in application. The present-day conception of a bishop as one with authority over a group of churches is a conception that took long to develop after the days of the apostles and the closing of the New Testament.

2. New Testament Co-operation and Apostolic Oversight.—It is true that there was co-operation among churches for benevolent purposes, but this was a voluntary co-operation. Paul's "care of all the churches" was not one of appointive authority. Paul was an apostle and the evangelist through whose efforts most of the churches referred to had been planted, but even then there is no suggestion of authority except such as applied naturally to his position as an apostle. Authoritative councils of metropolitan bishops appeared much later.

3. The Jerusalem Council.—True, there was a council in Jerusalem, but this was a case where local groups *asked* for counsel and guidance on special questions. They sought counsel from the assembled apostles and elders in Jerusalem in a day when they had not the written Word to which to turn, and they asked for this counsel from the very source which they should have consulted at that time and under the circumstances (Acts 15:2).

Even in this case the "apostles and elders" heard and discussed the matter, but did not use the words "command" or "order." They said that "we *write* unto them," etc. They were *asked* for counsel. The apostles *did have* authority from Jesus such as no one has today, though such is claimed by the pope. This writing, however, was no "ecclesiastical bull," but gracious counsel for which they had been asked. (See Acts 15:2, 4, 6, 19, 20, 22-29.)

4. Christ, the Only Head of the Church, and the Scriptures the Guide.—Acts 16:4 indicates, however, that these recommendations counted as "decrees" and authoritative, as well they might fittingly be counted, since they came from the apostles. If there were any councils or officials today having the same authority as the apostles had been given by the Lord, then, and then only, would there be ground for authoritative pronouncements to and authority over groups of churches. But, according to the New Testament, Christ is "head over all things pertaining to the church." *All* authority has been given unto Him, and His word and counsel are authoritatively given in the written Word of the New Testament.

IV. The New Testament Provision for Organization

New Testament organization was one that in each case grew out of a need. No officials were elected or appointed merely for the sake of organization. When needs arose, organization was expanded to fit the need.

1. Deacons.—While they were not at first designated as deacons, "seven men" were chosen by the members of the church in Jerusalem, "to have charge over this business." These were the first officials chosen, as far as the record goes. They were chosen to care for the distribution of contributions made for the needy brethren. The word *deakanos*, from which we get our word "deacon," meant "servant." The verb *diakonein* meant "to serve" or "minister to." Where the word appears a number of times in the New Testament it is translated variously as "deacon," "servant" and "minister."

References further on in the New Testament show that it became customary to choose deacons in the congregations. Their duty was *to serve.* Their qualifications for eligibility were high—men who had been *tried;* men *full of the Holy Spirit; grave, not double-tongued* (reliable and truthful); *sober; not money seekers; conscientious about the faith.*

2. Elders, Presbyters, Bishops or Pastors.—We have no New Testament history of the beginning of the eldership, but, apparently, the first elders were appointed by the apostles and evangelists. Even in this case there is every probability that these men were first chosen by the congregations following the Jerusalem precedent. (See Acts 14: 23; Tit. 1: 5.) Elder and presbyter mean "the older or more seasoned members"; bishop and pastor mean "shepherd and feeder of the flock."

(a) The ideal qualifications for eligibility to the eldership are:

> The bishop therefore must be without reproach, the husband of one wife, temperate, sober-minded, orderly, given to hospitality, apt to teach; no brawler, no striker; but gentle, not contentious,

no lover of money; one that ruleth well his own house, having his
children in subjection with all gravity; (but if a man knoweth
not how to rule his own house, how shall he take care of the church
of God?) not a novice, lest being puffed up he fall into the condemnation of the devil. Moreover, he must have good testimony
from them that are without; lest he fall into reproach and the
snare of the devil.—1 Tim. 3: 2-7, A.R.V.

(b) It will be recognized that quite probably not a single
soul has ever yet completely attained to this high standard. This is the standard, and naturally a standard of
measurement must represent the perfect. In choosing elders the members of the church should keep this standard
before them and conscientiously choose from their number those men who most nearly measure up to the standard. The Scriptures indicate, from the constant use of
the plural, that each congregation is to have a plurality
of elders or bishops. Apparently a one-man rule is
not contemplated.

(c) It will further be noted that of the fifteen points of the
standard only one has to do with authoritative ruling.
Mainly the authority is to be that derived from fitness,
ability and character.

3. Evangelists or Preachers.—Both these terms are used in
the New Testament, and are apparently meant as synonymous.
There is nothing in the Scriptures to indicate a distinction.
Either one is a proclaimer, i. e., a preacher of the Word, whether
in the local congregation or traveling to various fields. While
the Scriptures indicate that these are to be supported and
sustained by the church or churches, there is no Scriptural
sanction for setting them apart into a separate clerical class.
Distinctions between a "clergy" and "laity" are wholly foreign
to the New Testament. The terms "a divine" or "reverend"
as applied to a preacher are not to be found in the New Testament
and are apparently contrary to the teaching. The word "minister" is translated from the word *deakonos,* which means "ser-

vant.'' The preacher or evangelist is servant of Christ, and servant rather than master of the church. His place and work is to preach the Word in season and out of season.

> But be not ye called Rabbi: for one is your teacher, and all ye are brethren. And call no man your father on the earth: for one is your Father, even he who is in heaven. Neither be ye called masters: for one is your master, even the Christ. But he that is greatest among you shall be your servant. And whosoever shall exalt himself shall be humbled; and whosoever shall humble himself shall be exalted.—Matt. 23: 8-12, A.R.V.

V. Co-operation

The word ''co-operate'' comes from *co* plus *operari*, which means ''to work together.'' From Paul's letters we learn that these New Testament churches did work together to accomplish two things. They shared in relieving the needy and in sending messengers to spread the gospel. There is not the slightest indication, however, that this was done by or because of any compulsion or authoritative orders or by reason of any ecclesiastical officialdom over any group of churches. Each church or congregation was free in Christ and owned Him as not only chief authority, but as sole authority. The highest human authority rested in the elders, bishops, presbyters or pastors whose guidance or oversight or authority went no farther than the local congregation of which they were a part. This, of course, did not apply to the apostles who, during the temporary period of the founding of the church and the giving of the Word did have a divine authority given them by the Lord. There is no Scripture to indicate that this authority was to be transmitted on down and down in perpetuity other than as we have their written Word. That alone now represents the apostolic authority. That and that alone is of divine source. It alone voices God's will. That alone can be said to be infallible. No man is now authorized to speak for God. Christ and the Word are the final authority.

VI. A Summary

To summarize: The New Testament church today, since the passing of the apostles and prophets, consists of the saints or brethren or members or Christians. Among these and chosen from them are brethren who serve as elders (bishops, presbyters or pastors), others who serve as deacons (or deaconesses), others who are evangelists (preachers) and teachers. Christ is the sole *Head* of His church; the Word is final authority for its guidance in life and work.

The church is an "organism," rather than an organization, to carry on and carry out the work and mission of Christ the Lord.

The Son of man is come to seek and to save that which was lost.—Luke 19: 10.

As my Father hath sent me, even so send I you.—John 20: 21.

Every scripture inspired of God is also profitable for teaching, for reproof, for correction, for instruction which is in righteousness: that the man of God may be complete, furnished completely unto every good work.—2 Tim. 3: 16, 17, A.R.V.

The church of the New Testament as pictured in the inspired Word is an organism, solid in conviction, steadfast in faith, fervent in hope, patient in tribulation, sincere in righteousness, unselfish in endeavor and untiring in effort for the glory of Christ and the salvation of men everywhere.

QUESTIONS

1. What can you say as to the simplicity of the New Testament church organization?

2. What does "organization" mean?

3. What two phases of organization for a modern-day New Testament church would be legitimate?

4. Under what circumstances may added organization become wrong and harmful?

5. What are some of the dangerous tendencies in all human organizations?

6. Distinguish between an organization and an organism.

7. Illustrate how an organism functions.

8. What offices in the church are mentioned in the New Testament. Which ones were temporary and which remain as permanent?

9. How wide is the authority of the permanent offices mentioned in the New Testament?

10. What four terms are used in the New Testament to designate the office commonly designated as ''the eldership''?

11. What was the original meaning of the word translated ''deacon''?

12. What are the qualifications of a deacon?

13. What are the qualifications mentioned in the ideal standard for an elder?

14. Discuss the place and work of ''evangelists'' or ''preachers.''

15. Does the New Testament make provision for intercongregational co-operation?

16. Does the New Testament teaching suggest or justify ecclesiastical authority over any group of churches?

17. Summarize the New Testament description of a church of Christ.

Chapter XX

The Church and Its Divinely Given Task

I. CONFUSION IN THE CONCEPTIONS OF THE TASK OF THE CHURCH

There has probably been more confusion about the actual purpose, aim, place and task of the church than about any other one of its many phases. This is due quite apparently to men's tendency to add to or improve upon a divine plan. What is the task of the church?

Among the concepts as to its purpose, if we are to judge from actual observation today, are the following:

1. A great world-wide organization holding divine authority and with divinely commissioned power over the souls and destinies of men. This would be the Roman Catholic conception.

2. A world-wide organization which would be a combination of many denominations strong enough to exercise influence and pressure in matters social, political and ethical—an organization looking toward the alleviation of world social and political ills as well as the spiritual uplift of the masses. This would probably illustrate the conception of Protestant church federation movements of the day.

3. An organization whose primary purpose is wholly or largely eleemosynary, competing in such work with purely eleemosynary organizations in alleviating the ills of poverty, sickness, suffering and injustice. This is a more or less general and popular conception of the purpose of the church, especially by those outside the church.

4. An organization which is more a cultural society with a slant toward literary and philosophical preachments directed

toward ethical ends. This would possibly be best illustrated by Unitarianism and by individual congregations in many of the Protestant communions which have chosen pronouncedly modernistic leaders.

5. An organization for the teaching and preaching of a divinely given message, given for the spiritual redemption of individual men through the Christ the Son of the living God.

II. JESUS' CONCEPTIONS OF THE CHURCH

1. Jesus Christ, the Way.—Jesus indicated that His church should be founded and should rest on a great foundational and supernatural truth. That truth is that "Jesus is the Christ, the Son of the living God." That He is the Head and the only Head of the church and all things pertaining to it (Col. 1: 18; Eph. 1: 22). That He is "the way, the truth, and the life," and that "no man cometh unto the Father but by me" (Jesus) (John 14: 6). That He is "the resurrection, and the life: he that believeth on me, though he die, yet shall he live" (John 11: 25).

2. The Commission to the Church.—Jesus gave direct instruction to preach these truths and to tell men how to avail themselves of forgiveness and life.

All authority hath been given unto me in heaven and on earth. Go ye therefore, and make disciples of all the nations, baptizing them into the name of the Father and of the Son and of the Holy Spirit: teaching them to observe all things whatsoever I commanded you.—Matt. 28: 18-20, A.R.V.

Mark adds:

He that believeth and is baptized shall be saved; but he that disbelieveth shall be condemned.—Mark 16: 16, A.R.V.

3. Jesus Clearly Stated the Purpose.

The Son of man is come to seek and to save that which was lost.— Luke 19: 10, A.R.V.

As the Father hath sent me, even so send I you.—John 20: 21, A.R.V.

Here is most clearly defined the purpose of the church. When we forget the confusing conceptions of men about the church and seek only Jesus' conception, the matter becomes simple and clear.

III. THE APOSTLES' CONCEPTION OF THE CHURCH

If any one should have a clear conception of the church, its purpose and its mission, it would be the apostles who were personal companions of the Christ, were taught by Him and, finally, were inspired by the Holy Spirit sent by the Christ.

1. Peter's Conception of the Church and Its Mission.

(a) Pentecost. We have the record of Peter's presentation of the church in Acts 2. He preached Christ as the risen Lord. When they asked what to do he gave a clear-cut answer, "Repent ye, and be baptized every one of you in the name of Jesus Christ unto the remission of your sins." Then he recounted the promise and continued to exhort them with many words, saying, "Save yourselves from this crooked generation." This fitted in exactly with the picture of the church portrayed by Jesus.

(b) We may further gather an idea of Peter's conception from his Epistle.

> Blessed be the God and Father of our Lord Jesus Christ, which according to his abundant mercy hath begotten us again unto a lively hope by the resurrection of Jesus Christ from the dead, to an inheritance incorruptible, and undefiled, and that fadeth not away, reserved in heaven for you, who are kept by the power of God through faith unto salvation ready to be revealed in the last time.—1 Pet. 1: 3-5.

> Whereby he hath granted unto us his precious and exceeding great promises; that through these ye may become partakers of the divine nature, having escaped from the corruption that is in the world by lust. Yea, and for this very cause adding on your part all diligence, in your faith supply virtue; and in your virtue knowledge; and in your knowledge self-control; and in your self-

control patience; and in your patience godliness; and in your
godliness brotherly kindness; and in your brotherly kindness love.
For if these things are yours and abound, they make you to be
not idle nor unfruitful unto the knowledge of our Lord Jesus
Christ. For he that lacketh these things is blind, seeing only what
is near, having forgotten the cleansing from his old sins.—
2 Pet. 1: 4-9, A.R.V.

2. Paul's Conception of the Church and Its Mission.—Paul
was the great founder of churches. From his own pen we may
gather his conception of what made a church:

And I, brethren, when I came unto you, came not with excellency of
speech or of wisdom, proclaiming to you the testimony of God. For I
determined not to know anything among you, save Jesus Christ, and him
crucified.—1 Cor. 2: 1, 2, A.R.V.

But we preach Christ crucified, unto the Jews a stumblingblock, and
unto the Greeks foolishness; but unto them which are called, both Jews
and Greeks, Christ the power of God, and the wisdom of God.—1 Cor.
1: 23, 24.

For I delivered unto you first of all that which I also received, how
that Christ died for our sins according to the scriptures; and that he was
buried, and that he rose again the third day according to the scriptures:
. . . But if there be no resurrection of the dead, then is Christ not risen:
and if Christ be not risen, then is our preaching vain, and your faith is
also vain.—1 Cor. 15: 3, 4, 13, 14.

3. John's Conception of the Church and Its Mission.

Many other signs therefore did Jesus in the presence of the disciples,
which are not written in this book: but these are written, that ye may
believe that Jesus is the Christ, the Son of God; and that believing ye
may have life in his name.—John 20: 30, 31, A.R.V.

But as many as received him, to them gave he the right to become
children of God, even to them that believe on his name: who were born, not
of blood, nor of the will of the flesh, nor of the will of man, but of God.—
John 1: 12, 13, A.R.V.

For God so loved the world, that he gave his only begotten Son, that
whosoever believeth on him should not perish, but have eternal life. For
God sent not the Son into the world to judge the world; but that the
world should be saved through him. He that believeth on him is not
judged: he that believeth not hath been judged already, because he hath

not believed on the name of the only begotten Son of God.—John 3: 16-18, A.R.V.

If we say that we have fellowship with him and walk in the darkness, we lie, and do not the truth: but if we walk in the light, as he is in the light, we have fellowship one with another, and the blood of Jesus his Son cleanseth us from all sin.—1 John 1: 6, 7, A.R.V.

Whosoever believeth that Jesus is the Christ is begotten of God: and whosoever loveth him that begat loveth him also that is begotten of him. Hereby we know that we love the children of God, when we love God and do his commandments.—1 John 5: 1, 2, A.R.V.

These Scriptures give in brief the conceptions of the mission of the New Testament church. Here is shown what Jesus, Peter, Paul and John held as basic. The New Testament seems practically to take it for granted that he who hears the gospel of Christ, accepts Christ as Saviour, obeys Him as Lord, serves Him as Master and walks with Him as companion will ever strive to walk righteously and will unselfishly seek to serve his fellow man as against all ills, both individual and social.

IV. THE CHURCH AS A FIELD FOR SERVICE

The church is Christ's. The church has a definite mission, as we have seen. The church, by that reason, becomes Christ's field in which we are to work for Him for His reward.

Even as the Son of man came not to be ministered unto, but to minister.—Matt. 20: 28.

Lay up for yourselves treasures in heaven, where neither moth nor rust doth corrupt, and where thieves do not break through nor steal.—Matt. 6: 20.

V. GENERAL SUMMARY OF THE WHOLE MATTER

The New Testament church, the church of Christ, is His church. He is its one and only Saviour, He is the one and only Head, He is the Founder and sole Owner. Christ, through the Holy Spirit, established the church. No man or group of men ever were commissioned to add to, take from or change that which Christ established. The New Testament is the one and only divine record of Christ's church. To be allowed to belong to the church of Christ is the world's greatest blessing. It is the field of Christ in the world in which we may serve Him for the reward of forgiveness of sin and eternal life. Christ, being the only Saviour, could and did lay down the conditions upon which these blessings are granted and which are identical with the conditions of becoming a member of His body—His church. These conditions are:

1. Hearing and heeding His Word.
2. Believing His Word.
3. Sincere repentance or yielding to His will.
4. Confession of our faith in Him with our mouths before men.
5. Baptism into Christ.
6. A life consecrated in loyalty to and service for Christ.
7. Perseverance through all vicissitudes.

QUESTIONS

1. Give a number of the theological and popular conceptions of the place and purpose of the church.

2. Summarize the New Testament picture of the church as to its purpose and work.

3. On what one great foundational truth did Christ say His church should rest?

4. Quote the Great Commission given in Matt. 28: 18-20, and show how this links with the one foundational truth.

5. Quote a Scripture in which Jesus clearly and briefly states the purpose of His coming.

6. Quote a Scripture showing that the purpose He had for the church is to carry out His aim and purpose.

7. Show how Peter's sermon on Pentecost fits directly with this same purpose.

8. Show from Peter's writings that he clung definitely to the truth that Jesus is the Christ as proven by His death and resurrection.

9. Outline the elements of Christian growth as given by Peter.

10. What constituted the heart of Paul's preaching?

11. What was John's basic theme and the one purpose of his Gospel?

12. Show that the church is Christ's field for our Christian labors.

13. Summarize the New Testament teachings as to Christ's church.